PRAISE FOR

# The Next Level

*"Gives thoughtful and practical insight into the 'how-to' of being a leader—one who constantly makes a positive change—not just a manager in an organization."*

> —CATHERINE A. MELOY, PRESIDENT/CEO, GOODWILL OF GREATER WASHINGTON; FORMER SENIOR VICE PRESIDENT, CLEAR CHANNEL COMMUNICATIONS

*"An outstanding primer concerning what it takes to move up and excel in executive leadership positions. A superb leadership development tool and a must-read for both existing and up-and-coming executives."*

> —MAJOR GENERAL (RET.) STEPHEN T. RIPPE, EXECUTIVE VICE PRESIDENT & COO, PROTESTANT EPISCOPAL CATHEDRAL FOUNDATION

*"An easy-to-understand, concise guide providing practical advice and insight on the requirements for successful behaviors and skills as an executive. A great reference for any executive."*

> —AMR ELSAWY, SENIOR VICE PRESIDENT, MITRE

# The Next Level

# The
# Next
# Level

WHAT INSIDERS KNOW ABOUT

EXECUTIVE SUCCESS

# Scott Eblin

**Davies-Black Publishing**
Mountain View, California

Published by Davies-Black Publishing, a division of CPP, Inc., 1055 Joaquin Road, 2nd Floor, Mountain View, CA 94043; 800-624-1765.

Special discounts on bulk quantities of Davies-Black books are available to corporations, professional associations, and other organizations. For details, contact the Director of Marketing and Sales at Davies-Black Publishing: 650-691-9123; fax 650-623-9271.

Visit the Davies-Black Publishing Web site at www.daviesblack.com.

10 09 08 07 06    10 9 8 7 6 5 4 3 2
Printed in the United States of America

**Library of Congress Cataloging-in-Publication Data**
Eblin, Scott
The next level : what insiders know about executive success / Scott Eblin.
    p. cm.
Includes index.
ISBN-13: 978-0-89106-193-9 (hardcover)
ISBN-10: 0-89106-193-2
1. Executives. 2. Executive ability. 3. Success. I. Title.
HD38.2.E25 2006
658.4'09—dc22

                  2006006017

FIRST EDITION
First printing 2006

To Diane, my partner and inspiration

# CONTENTS

**Preface  xi**

**Acknowledgments  xv**

**About the Author  xix**

**1    Advancing Through Uncharted Terrain  1**

── **Part 1** ════════════════════════════════════════
**THE FOUNDATIONS OF PERSONAL PRESENCE**

**2    Pick Up Confidence in Your Presence  19**
Let Go of Doubt in How You Contribute

**3    Pick Up Regular Renewal of Your Energy
and Perspective  41**
Let Go of Running Flat Out Until You Crash

**4    Pick Up Custom-Fit Communications  61**
Let Go of One-Size-Fits-All Communications

## Part 2
## THE FOUNDATIONS OF TEAM PRESENCE

**5  Pick Up Team Reliance  87**
Let Go of Self-Reliance

**6  Pick Up Defining What to Do  103**
Let Go of Telling How to Do It

**7  Pick Up Accountability for Many Results  119**
Let Go of Responsibility for a Few Results


## Part 3
## THE FOUNDATIONS OF ORGANIZATIONAL PRESENCE

**8  Pick Up Looking Left and Right as You Lead  137**
Let Go of Looking Primarily Up and Down as You Lead

**9  Pick Up an Outside-In View of the Entire Organization  159**
Let Go of an Inside-Out View of Your Function

**10  Pick Up a Big-Footprint View of Your Role  173**
Let Go of a Small-Footprint View of Your Role

**Afterword: Living at the Next Level  191**

**Appendix A: Create Your Executive Success Plan™ (ESP™) 195**

**Appendix B: Situation Solutions Guide  201**

**Index  213**

# PREFACE

Certain moments stay with you through the years. One of those moments for me came in the televised debate of candidates for vice president in 1992. The major party candidates that year were Dan Quayle and Al Gore. There was a third-party candidate as well—the late retired admiral James Stockdale, who was the running mate of the Reform party nominee, Ross Perot. Less than twenty years before, Stockdale had received the Congressional Medal of Honor for his leadership and sacrifice as the highest-ranking prisoner at the Hanoi Hilton during the Vietnam War. Through a series of unexpected events, Stockdale found himself in 1992 running for vice president.

At the beginning of the debate, each candidate was given the opportunity to make some introductory remarks; Stockdale went last. His opening statement began with two questions, "Who am I?"

and "Why am I here?" As the debate unfolded, Stockdale never really got the chance to answer those questions, and he later acknowledged that he was unprepared for the debate—having found out only twelve days before the fact that there was even going to be a debate for the vice presidential candidates. Given his background, there is no doubt that under different circumstances and in a different context, Stockdale could have eloquently answered his questions with personal stories about leadership and courage.

As a senior officer in an enemy prison camp, Stockdale faced one of the ultimate tests of advancing through uncharted terrain. He never knew what the next day would bring and when, or if, he would get out of the situation alive. In an interview with Jim Collins for *Good to Great,* Stockdale said the prisoners who eventually survived the Hanoi Hilton had at least three things in common. First, they were clear and honest with themselves about the reality of the situation. Second, they picked up a belief that they would get out alive. Third, they let go of any hope of getting out by a particular date. Stockdale told Collins that the prisoners who didn't survive were the ones who told themselves they would be out by a date over which they had no control, such as Christmas or their child's birthday. The date would come and go with no release and these prisoners would eventually lose hope and die.

While most of us will never face an experience as terrible as imprisonment in the Hanoi Hilton, we will all, like Stockdale and his comrades, be faced at different times in our lives with the challenge of advancing through uncharted terrain. We can learn a lot from them about how they approached this journey. They relied first on characteristics such as courage and a willingness to face reality that defined who they were at their best. They picked up beliefs and behaviors that moved them forward. They let go of beliefs and behaviors that held them back.

When I set out to write this book, my goal was to provide a resource for new executive leaders advancing into the uncharted terrain of the next career level. My belief that moving to the executive level is among the toughest transitions of any career is borne out by the statistics. According to research conducted by Manchester Associates, 40 percent of new executives fail within eighteen months of being named to their positions. What's going on here? Is it a case of the Peter Principle at work? Have 40 percent of all new executives simply risen to their level of incompetence? That seems unlikely. After all, to get to the executive level, you usually have to be pretty smart, accomplished, and competent. How to explain the sudden increase in the failure rate once leaders reach the executive suite?

Let's look first at expectations. Based on my experience as an executive and coach in Fortune 500 corporations, I know that the expectations of performance for new executives are very high. I also know that they are very rarely explicitly stated. Unfortunately, much of the time the only expectation that is shared with new executives is that they are to figure out what to do and how to do it. Through interviews with more than thirty successful executives, I have written this book to serve as a road map of the often unstated expectations faced by new executive leaders. Through my research, I have defined nine sets of key behaviors and beliefs that new executives need to pick up and let go of to succeed. This process of picking up and letting go, I've learned, is central to succeeding at the executive level.

The competence that propels leaders to the executive level can be both a blessing and a curse. There is a truth in executive coaching and leadership development that a strength when overused can become a weakness. It turns out that many new executives overuse and overrely on the technical competence that served them so well earlier in their careers. A theme that came up again and again in my interviews with successful executives is that moving to the next level requires the courage and confidence to let go of some of the things that brought you there. Peak performance in the uncharted terrain of the next level demands that you identify and rely on the characteristics that describe how you are at your best. Knowing what to do is important, but knowing how you are at your best and creating the conditions to perform from that state are more important.

Possessing the confidence that comes from understanding how you are at your best can serve as the basis for making the choices that need to be made in any situation that calls for advancing through uncharted terrain. In a world of continuous change, this is an invaluable attribute to have. Operating from that base of confidence in yourself will enable you to have the clarity of thought needed to make smart strategic choices about what you need to pick up—and what you must let go—as you advance into the uncharted terrain of the next level of your career.

# ACKNOWLEDGMENTS

Having read or at least skimmed hundreds of books over the years, I have long been intrigued by the authors' acknowledgments. How, I have often wondered, can it be possible that so many people need to be acknowledged and thanked for their contributions to one book? Now that I have written a book, I know! The number of people who have directly and indirectly influenced the content of *The Next Level* surprises even me. Please allow me to take a few pages to express my gratitude and appreciation for these individuals' support and involvement in this book.

The book benefited greatly from the insights of more than two dozen executives who graciously allowed me to interview them. In addition to the few who requested anonymity for their comments, I want to thank Cathy Abbott, Lucien Alziari, Martin Carter, Stephen

Cerrone, Bill Christopher, Marc Effron, Sid Fuchs, Mary Good, Jason Jeffay, Bob Johnson, Mike Lanier, David Levy, Steve Linehan, Henry Lucas, Jay Marmer, Paul McDermott, Catherine Meloy, Donna Morea, Kathleen O'Leary, Laura Olle, Bill Plamondon, Joni Reich, Steve Rippe, Ed Sannini, and Steve Smith for their contributions to *The Next Level*. Each of these leaders influenced my thinking and the direction of this book. Since I conducted the interviews in 2004 and early 2005, a number of them have moved on to other organizations. The titles and affiliations noted here reflect the roles of the interviewees at the time at which I spoke with them.

I have been blessed with the support of many other friends and colleagues who were instrumental in helping me turn an idea into a book. Marla Bobowick was a godsend in guiding me through the first several drafts of my book proposal. Catherine Fitzgerald was incredibly generous with her advice on publishing and in providing an introduction to my publisher, Davies-Black. Vickie Sullivan was a creative spark and source of motivation in thinking about the broader applications of this material. My phenomenal assistant, Laura Pumo, did her usual fantastic job in managing the administrative aspects of my business and in helping me manage my time so I could continue to serve my clients while working on the book. As the manuscript took shape, a number of colleagues read excerpts and provided helpful feedback. Four people in particular, Amr ElSawy, Mark Joseph, Jenny Tucker, and Holly Williams, went above and beyond the call of duty by reading the entire manuscript and providing incredibly helpful advice that improved the end product.

Thanks also to the many clients, colleagues, and friends who introduced me to a number of the executives I interviewed. Their support and participation was invaluable. Finally, to Wayne and the baristas at Starbucks #7606, thank you for keeping the drinks, food, music, and welcome diversions coming while I camped out at your place on the weekends when I was writing the manuscript. There aren't many restaurants in which you can take over a table for hours on end without feeling pressured to hurry up and close out the check!

The more I learn about publishing, the more I realize how fortunate I am to be associated with my publisher, Davies-Black. My editor, Connie Kallback, has been a consistent source of good advice and encouragement. Laura Simonds has been an enthusiastic partner in thinking about how to get *The Next Level* to the readers who will benefit from it. Jill Anderson-Wilson has been a pleasure to work with in fine-tuning the book editorially. All of these folks and the rest of the team at Davies-Black have been very open during this process and have asked for and listened to my ideas. Thank you for viewing me as your partner. With all the help I've had from so many people, any mistakes or opportunities for improvement in this book are, at this point, solely my responsibility.

Each of us is a product of the people we have met who influenced us along the way. I could not begin to count the people who have had a positive impact on what I have to offer the world and the way in which I offer it. Deep thanks goes to each of them; they have made a difference in my life. In connecting the dots that led to this book, there are a number of people I want to single out for a specific word of appreciation. I have had the good fortune of working for and learning from a diverse range of senior executives in my career. To Peter Johnson, Gaston Caperton, Phyllis Arnold, Holmes Morrison, and especially Cathy Abbott, thank you for believing in me, often giving me more responsibility than I was ready for, and for teaching me how to be an executive. To my personal coaches over the years, Marc Sokol, Deborah Dickerson, Julie Shows, Nancy Baker, and Chris Wahl, thank you for asking powerful questions and listening to my answers. To Nancy Collamer and Mike McDermott, thank you for providing the spark and the kindling for my career as a coach and executive advisor. To my colleagues in the Alliance for Strategic Leadership, the leadership coaching certificate program of

Georgetown University, and the broader coaching community, thank you for your generosity of spirit and the food for thought. To the many wonderful clients I have had over the years, thank you for the opportunity to learn from you and to admire the ways in which you lead.

My greatest blessing is the family that provided for me as a child and that I provide for as an adult. Because of them, I have had many amazing opportunities, including the experience of writing this book. My dad and mom, Jack and Judy Eblin, provided the foundation of love and support I needed to go in the directions that best suited me and that played to my natural strengths. Through his example, my brother, Steve, has taught me about the value of friendship and honoring commitments. Thanks to each of you for the support given and the lessons learned. My sons, Andy and Brad, are a continuous source of joy, growth, and perspective. They are both blessings. Thank you for being the young men that you are and for your patience with me when work sometimes intrudes. Finally, my wife, Diane, is the greatest gift I have been or will be given. My hope and prayer for anyone reading this book is that they be blessed with a partner who believes in them, encourages them, dreams with them, and loves them unconditionally. I have all of that in Diane, and I thank God for her each day.

# ABOUT THE AUTHOR

Scott Eblin draws on his experience as a nationally recognized Fortune 500 executive innovator to advise leaders on succeeding at the next level. As president of The Eblin Group, he works with clients nationally and internationally to help them successfully navigate the changing landscape of leadership. He currently coaches and advises executives in such organizations as AOL, Capital One, Northrop Grumman, Sallie Mae, Sanofi-Aventis, and The World Bank.

Eblin has more than twenty years of experience as an advisor and coach to the senior leadership of diverse organizations in the private, public, and nonprofit sectors. Prior to forming his own firm, he served as vice president of human resources for the largest division of a Fortune 500 energy company. In that role, he implemented change management strategies that helped transform the division from a bankrupt, command-and-control utility company to one that was customer focused, employee oriented, and an industry leader in profitability. For its work, Eblin's HR department was recognized as among the most innovative in a national competition.

While Eblin's experience extends across a broad range of organizations and situations, the common denominator in his career is a unique ability to help organizations achieve strategic goals by building the capacity of their leaders. Among his career highlights is serving as the youngest vice president of a rapidly growing financial services company, which was named by *U.S. Banker* as one of the nation's ten best large banks. His experience in the public sector includes service with the governor of West Virginia as the lead executive in charge of an initiative to develop grassroots leadership for economic growth. Early in his career, Eblin led a program sponsored by the Council of the Americas to build the leadership of chambers of commerce in developing countries in the Caribbean Basin. He also worked in the public finance division of a leading Wall Street investment bank.

Eblin graduated with honors from Davidson College with a degree in international relations. He also holds an MPA degree from Harvard University. He is a graduate of Georgetown University's leadership coaching certificate program and also serves on the program faculty. He is a professional certified coach and a member of the International Coach Federation.

Eblin lives with his wife and two sons in the Washington, D.C., suburbs of northern Virginia. He can be reached via e-mail through www.eblingroup.com.

# ADVANCING THROUGH UNCHARTED TERRAIN

Congratulations! You've just been promoted to the executive ranks of your organization. Alternatively, you've been told that within the next six to twelve months you should be promoted to this level. Or perhaps you're already an executive and your role is changing. Any of these events is a major milestone in your career and merits a bit of reflection on what brought you this far.

If you're like most of your peers, your path to the executive level has probably run from a starting point as the stellar individual contributor on a team. You may have then been promoted to manage that team on a day-to-day basis, making sure that the team's work was brought in on time and exceeded expectations. In your company, the executive level may begin when you are responsible for overseeing the work of multiple teams. That may be where you are now or soon will be. Or, it may be that entry into the executive team of your company comes when you are responsible for a major profit center or enterprise-wide support function like finance or human resources. For the purposes of this book, I'll define an *executive level role* as one that reports directly to the company president or one that reports to a direct report of the president. If you are working in a major subsidiary of a Fortune 1000 corporation and you report to the subsidiary president you are probably considered to be an executive, at least in the context of your subsidiary. If you are in such a role or are reporting directly to a senior executive in a smaller company, you are in the target audience for this book.

If you're fortunate, you have had one or more mentors along the way who have guided and counseled you on what it takes to be successful at the different levels through which you have already moved. Perhaps you still have such a mentor and your transition to the next level will be smooth, hassle-free, and completely successful. If you are so blessed, you probably don't need this book. If you are in the 99 percent of the corporate population without this extra measure of exceedingly good fortune, read on for advice and truth from highly successful executives who collectively will be your mentor and guide to successfully advancing through the uncharted terrain of the next level.

## The Learning Continuum

As a former Fortune 500 human resources executive and current executive coach, I have had a lot of direct and vicarious experience with transitions to the executive level. I have seen a few smooth transitions to the top, a lot of bumpy ones, and more than a few flame-outs. Over the past several years, I've concluded that moving successfully to the executive level requires conscious intent about what behaviors and beliefs to keep as well as what behaviors and beliefs to pick up and let go. The bumps I experienced in my own executive transition, as well as those I've seen in colleagues and clients, were rooted in two distinct phases of the learning continuum. The first phase is when you literally don't know what you don't know—otherwise called *unconscious incompetence.* Based on the theory that ignorance is bliss, you might actually enjoy this phase. After all, you've just been named an executive and life is good!

If you're lucky, phase one will last a week or two before phase two begins. This is that painful period of *conscious incompetence* when you begin to discern that there are things you need to know that you don't know. However bad continued incompetence may sound, at least you're making progress in advancing through this new terrain. In all likelihood, if you're going to be incompetent, it's better to be conscious than unconscious!

## Moving Toward Competence

The purpose of this book is to guide you as a new executive in moving very quickly through the two phases of incompetence to the next two phases of learning. These are *conscious competence,* in which you know what you need to know but it doesn't yet come completely naturally, and *unconscious competence,* in which you know what you need to know, you're good at it, and you're operating at your best with ease.

Before we go any further, let's touch on an obvious point. You are likely a highly competent and functional human being or you would not have made it as far you have. You are, however, entering a new phase in your career—and, to sustain your success, you will have to let go of some beliefs and behaviors that have been working for you until now. You will also have to pick up some new beliefs and behaviors to achieve success as an executive. Based on my experience as an executive and a coach, I have some assessments of my own about what you should pick up and let go, but if I were you I would want more than one person's opinions. So I have enlisted around thirty accomplished senior executives to share their perspectives on what to pick up and let go of to be a successful executive. Collectively, they will guide you to executive success.

● ● ●

## Amy: Case Study of a New Executive

Before we get to their advice, let's consider the case of Amy, who has just been promoted to vice president for product development.

*Amy has been a star performer for her financial services company since she arrived five years ago, after a three-year stint as an associate in a major management consulting firm. Amy moved from being a key contributor on a product development team to becoming the leader of that team after two and a half years. One year after that, she became a director with responsibility for a couple of key product lines.*

*As a director, Amy continued to deliver what her senior vice president had come to expect of her. She was a brilliant analyst with a gift for sifting through data and making grounded predictions on new products that would appeal to the high-income, high-balance customers that were the target of her business segment. In her director role, Amy enhanced her reputation as someone who stayed on top of every detail and who, when her team members were stuck or headed in the wrong direction, could provide the right solution to drive progress forward. Her energy and focus enabled her to work ten or eleven hours a day at the office, which she usually supplemented with an hour or two responding to e-mail and voice mail most evenings. Her weekends typically incorporated at least five or six hours of work-related reading and planning for the upcoming week. Because of her single-minded focus on product development, Amy spent most of her time dealing with members of her team and did not have a lot of space left over for networking with peers and business leaders outside her domain of expertise. This lack of broader exposure created a bit of a challenge for her senior vice president when he recommended Amy for promotion to the executive ranks, but, in the end, the results she had delivered over the past several years carried the day, and she was named a vice president of the company.*

*Amy has been a vice president for four months now and feels like she is paddling hard to keep her head above water. With the vice president's title has come responsibility for three new product lines in addition to the two she grew and now oversees. With five key product lines to keep track of, she is finding that she is working longer and longer hours and is still not able to stay on top of all the details.*

*A number of factors are driving up her hours—some expected and some unexpected. Amy has not been surprised that the broader scope of her responsibilities has increased the amount of attention she has to give to her now-expanded team. Because Amy is an expert in her field, she has made a practice of stepping in to provide detailed suggestions to her team members on how to solve problems they face on their projects. To her chagrin and puzzlement, she has found that her newer direct reports will often take the ideas that she comes up with when she is "just thinking out loud" and implement them without her even realizing that she had given them the idea. Some of the results of this phenomenon have been less than optimal and have required her time to step in and correct the problems that were created.*

*Another thing Amy did not expect was how much time she would spend preparing for the weekly meetings that her senior vice president has with her and his three other VPs. She is exquisitely aware that he expects her and the other VPs to have a strong handle on what is going on in their areas and to be able to speak to their issues whenever he asks. He also expects his direct reports to offer insights and advice on each other's responsibilities. Amy is spending several hours each week gathering the information she thinks she might need for the SVP's staff meetings. It feels to her like getting ready for a pop quiz each week.*

*Amy is beginning to notice other factors that are contributing to the complexity of her new job. As her team has grown, she has inherited a number of new direct reports. One of these, Brian, consistently disappoints Amy with both the quality of his work and the negative attitude he regularly exhibits. He has a reputation for being technically brilliant and probably considered himself a candidate for the slot that is now Amy's. More and more, Amy is finding that she has to follow up with Brian to make sure that he delivers on his commitments. On more than one occasion, she has been blindsided by important decisions that Brian has made but has not shared with her. With what little time she has had to think through the situation, Amy is beginning to conclude that Brian may not be a fit for her team, but she is reluctant to take on the time and hassle of putting together a game plan for dealing with him. For now, she's hoping that he'll turn around on his own.*

*Adding to the pressure is Amy's recognition that her boss also expects her to have a grounded point of view on how to drive revenue growth for the company as a whole, not just in her product lines. This expectation was further brought home in Amy's first quarterly business review (QBR) with her boss and the company CEO and the rest of his directs. In preparing for that session, Amy had her staff working for weeks on a thirty-slide PowerPoint® deck that she intended to present to the top executive team. When it came time for her to speak, she sensed that she was losing the group about three slides into her deck. She sped through the next several slides, skipped some in the middle and attempted to salvage her main points as she jumped ahead to the summary slide. Amy left her first QBR with her confidence shaken. Other than what she said in her presentation, she had not participated in the conversation around the table and, frankly, felt like an imposter who was playing at a level for which she was not yet ready.*

*Although he does not consider her an imposter, Amy's boss is concerned about her performance and that of her broader team since she was named a vice president. He is surprised that her performance seems to be declining and is wondering if Amy's promotion was perhaps a case of offering her too much too soon.*

● ● ●

## What Should Amy Do?

Clearly, Amy is going through a rough stretch. Almost as clear is the fact that she is not getting a lot of support and guidance from her boss. High-performers are often elevated to the executive level and then left to figure out on their own how to operate successfully in their new roles. For executives, the expectations are high but rarely stated explicitly. Let's take some time to assume the role of Amy's coach and help her identify some changes she needs to make to get back to the high level of performance that she has had in her career up to this point.

### Have Confidence in Her Presence

Amy has to brush off the jitters that have shaken her confidence as a new executive and adopt the belief that she should be exactly where she is. One of the first challenges for many new executives is to let go of the idea that the succession plan must have had some sort of fluke that led to their arrival in the executive suite. In Amy's case, as it often is for new executives, this uncertainty is compounded by the challenge of advancing through the uncharted terrain of moving from unconscious incompetence to unconscious competence.

Even as she is moving through the unknown, it is important for her to remember that there are sound reasons why she has been selected for her new role. Amy needs to believe that she has been invited to the table because she is expected to contribute in meaningful ways. This belief should come through in the way she presents herself to her colleagues. Executive presence relies on adopting a relaxed confidence that puts others at ease and instills confidence in your judgment. It requires that you silence any inner critics that call into question whether you are ready for your role or deserve your shot as an executive leader. Amy does have tactical opportunities to build her confidence on a day-to-day basis (as you probably do, too). There are also transformational opportunities to strengthen your executive presence so that it is a natural extension of how you are at your best. Both the tactical and transformational opportunities will be addressed in this book.

## Be Accountable Instead of Responsible for Results

As an objective observer, you most likely concluded that Amy has unrealistic expectations about her ability and need to be directly involved in everything that is going on in her area. As an individual contributor and as a functional manager, Amy was responsible for delivering specific projects or streams of work. As an executive, she is now accountable for seeing that others meet their responsibilities for deliverables.

The difference between responsibility and accountability is the difference between doing and leading. Too many new executives continue to spend time acting directly in the realm of their functional expertise because they are comfortable in the space that has made them successful to date. As an executive, Amy is on the hook for what her people get done. She cannot allow herself to be on the hook for doing it all herself if she hopes to meet the broader expectations built into her new role.

## Define What, Not How

Closely related to the issue of confusing responsibility with accountability is Amy's habit of stepping in to provide detailed solutions to
the challenges facing her team members. Amy's approach poses a
number of problems. First, with the increased scope of her responsibilities, Amy simply does not have the time to be the go-to person on
every issue and still meet her obligations as an executive. Second,
and just as important, by always providing the solution, Amy is limiting the development of both her team members and her team leaders. One of Amy's key functions as an executive is to help build the
next generation of leaders for her company, and she's missing out on
one of the best means of fulfilling this expectation, which is to define
the results that are needed but not how to get those results. Again,
as an executive, Amy is accountable for the results her team pro-
duces; they are responsible for producing the results. Her job is to
define what the results should be, not how to accomplish the results.

## Look Left and Right as She Leads

To put her performance back on track, Amy needs to recognize and
respond to the things that have changed now that she is an executive.
One of the most significant changes, and opportunities, that has been
created by her promotion is that Amy is now part of a new team—
the executive team. Amy needs to be intentional and deliberate
about looking left and right to collaborate with her new executive
peers. As an executive, Amy has more access than she did a few
months ago. If she chooses to take advantage of her access, she has
valuable opportunities to partner with her peers in other functions to
contribute to the broader business agenda of her company. In turn,
she can bring a broader and more grounded perspective back to her
functional team, enabling them to better understand how their
actions support the goals of the company. No one else on her functional team has the kind of access that Amy now has. She is the only

one who can apply those aspects of the broader view that she can take as the vice president for product development. Amy needs to develop some new habits around taking the opportunity to collaborate with her peers.

## Take the Outside-In View

Amy has many clear strengths, and one of the most notable is her tenacity in delivering on her commitments. Over the years she has come to be known as someone who lets nothing get in the way of delivering the results expected of her function. Unfortunately, she has become a living illustration of the truth that an overused strength can become a weakness. Amy's focus on her functional work has damaged her peripheral vision. Over the past few years, she has not left herself much time for forming and growing relationships with people who can give her fresh perspectives on important company issues or offer advice and counsel on key opportunities to which she should pay attention. She needs to restructure her time and perspective so she can more clearly see what is important to the business as a whole and how her function fits into that bigger picture.

## Develop a Big-Footprint View of Her Role

As an executive, Amy needs to learn that she has acquired a bigger footprint in the organization and, as such, her words and actions carry more impact and consequence than they used to. When used well, this big footprint will allow her to get more done through others and accomplish more for her company. She needs to learn, though, that, because many people in the organization will want to move quickly in order to make a good impression on her as an executive, her words and actions can have unintended consequences. This is what's causing the problems Amy is experiencing with her new direct reports' tendency to act too quickly.

At the same time that she is learning to manage her new profile with respect to her subordinates, she will need to step up to the expectations of other executives in the company. To be successful as an executive, Amy will have to quickly develop a point of view around value creation and show conviction in expressing it. Being grounded in a point of view about your discipline is the price of admission to the executive team. Once you're on the team, you distinguish yourself by presenting that point of view in a way that interacts with other disciplines to move the organization forward. For a new executive like Amy, quarterly business reviews with the CEO and weekly staff meetings with senior executives are important forums for showing conviction and a bias for action around a well-reasoned point of view.

## Develop Team Reliance

Amy is finding that she is in constant motion attempting to stay on top of what her expanded team is doing and directing their work. While she may not realize it, part of Amy's challenge is to get her ego out of the way and let go of the idea that she is the only one who can ensure that the right work gets done in the right way. In the past, Amy has derived satisfaction from her personal accomplishments on the job, but now she needs to shift the source of that satisfaction to what her team accomplishes. To trust that her team will do the right work in the right way, she needs to move quickly to ensure that she has the right people on the team in terms of both their motivation and their ability to contribute. In this regard, she needs to resolve the situation with Brian by either obtaining his commitment to contribute fully to the work of the team or helping him find a situation that better meets her needs and his.

## Custom-Fit Her Communications

The episode that brought Amy's situation to a boil with her boss was her performance in the quarterly business review with the company CEO. Needless to say, highly visible events such as a QBR merit preparation and forethought from any executive. In Amy's case, her preparation went into a finely crafted PowerPoint deck when that time likely would have been better spent on other aspects of her performance in the meeting. In preparing for meetings with senior executives and other key stakeholders, Amy needs to develop the habit of asking herself questions such as these:

- Who is the audience for my message?

- Where are they now in terms of their thinking?

- What, if anything, do I need to do to change their thinking?

When making a presentation or the case for a new initiative, Amy should assess who is going to be in the audience and get clear about what she wants them to think and how she wants them to feel after she speaks. What is the emotional response that will lead to the appropriate action? Does she need the audience to feel excited? Concerned? Optimistic? Challenged? She should shape the content of her message, her body language, and her tone of voice to create the response that leads to the best action by the members of the group. There is a lot Amy can do to master the art of tuning in to the audience.

## Regularly Renew Energy and Perspective

My guess is you probably felt fatigued just reading about all that is going on in Amy's world. Let's shift the focus then, from Amy to you. Ron Heifetz, professor at Harvard University and author of *Leadership Without Easy Answers,* makes the point that leaders periodically need to get off the dance floor and up on the balcony. By making this shift, you can see the patterns and the flow better than when they're right in front of you. One of the best ways to get up on the balcony is to establish routines of renewal that you regularly practice.

Life as an executive is demanding and it requires your best. To succeed over the long run as an executive, you will need to pick up routines of renewal in the mental, physical, spiritual, and relational domains of your life. You've likely reached the executive level in part because of your commitment and drive. Now that you're here, don't overdo it. Your energy and perspective will serve you well in the uncharted terrain of the next level if you establish space in your life to reinforce and reconnect with how you are at your best.

## Follow Your ESP™

By encouraging you to Follow your ESP™, I am not recommending that you develop an obsession with your sixth sense. Rather, I would encourage you, Amy, or any executive to establish an Executive Success Plan™. In reading through Amy's case, it is easy to become overwhelmed with the number of things that she needs to address. There is no way she can address all her opportunities at once. She needs to pick the one or two most important opportunities that, over a forty-five- to ninety-day period, will have the biggest positive ripple effect on how she shows up as an executive. She then needs to identify one or two more things to work on and repeat the cycle. I will confess that in writing Amy's case, I purposely gave her a lot of problems to address in order to illustrate the major points that our senior executive mentors share in the rest of this book. Whether you are a new or more seasoned executive, I am reasonably certain that you have opportunities for improvement that you can address. I seriously doubt, however, that you have as many as Amy. Appendix A introduces a process and framework for building your Executive Success Plan by soliciting feedback from your colleagues and enlisting them to be your team of coaches committed to your success as a new executive.

## Anatomy of *The Next Level*

I want to take a moment to explain how the rest of the book is organized. Each of the following chapters focuses on one of nine pairs of behaviors and beliefs that one must pick up and let go of to be a successful executive. These pairs of behaviors and beliefs deal with the issues outlined in the case study on Amy. Each chapter concludes with a summary list of ten tips for picking up the different elements of executive presence. You'll notice that the nine pick-up-and-let-go distinctions are organized into three broad components of executive presence: personal presence, team presence and organizational presence. When the Next Level model of executive presence is put together, it looks like the one shown in the following chart. Because executive development is an ongoing journey, this book contains two features in the appendices that will be useful to your growth as a leader. The first is the previously mentioned template for creating an Executive Success Plan (see Appendix A). The second is a Situation Solutions Guide (see Appendix B), which identifies typical situations in which you may find yourself as an executive and the solutions from each chapter that can help.

Again, congratulations on your appointment as an executive. I look forward, in the pages to come, to being your guide in making the strategic choices around what to pick up and let go of to ensure your success as you advance through the uncharted terrain of the next level.

## BUILDING EXECUTIVE PRESENCE

| Pick Up | Let Go Of |
|---|---|
| **PERSONAL PRESENCE** | |
| Confidence in your presence | Doubt in how you contribute |
| Regular renewal of your energy and perspective | Running flat out until you crash |
| Custom-fit communications | One-size-fits-all communications |
| **TEAM PRESENCE** | |
| Team reliance | Self-reliance |
| Defining what to do | Telling how to do it |
| Accountability for many results | Responsibility for a few results |
| **ORGANIZATIONAL PRESENCE** | |
| Looking left and right as you lead | Looking primarily up and down as you lead |
| An outside-in view of the entire organization | An inside-out view of your function |
| A big-footprint view of your role | A small-footprint view of your role |

**PART 1**

# The Foundations of
# Personal Presence

# 2

## PICK UP CONFIDENCE IN YOUR PRESENCE

## LET GO OF DOUBT IN HOW YOU CONTRIBUTE

Let's start with a basic truth: Insecure people make lousy leaders. If you think about your career, you can probably identify at least one or two managers you've had who exhibited insecurity. Their insecurity may have shown up in any number of ways. They may have been indecisive when major issues needed to be resolved. They didn't trust their judgment or were afraid of the consequences that would result from making a clear and, perhaps, unpopular decision. Or insecurity may have been at the root of their need to micromanage and control the work of everyone on their team. If this was the situation, then your manager probably worked round the clock trying to stay on top of every detail. In the meantime, of course, the team's work slowed down or regularly stopped as it waited for the bottleneck on the manager's desk to clear. Perhaps you've worked for a leader who claimed credit for every good thing that happened but was quick to pass blame when things went wrong. Here again, the root cause was the manager's insecurity. Let's face it, if you've been a participant in organizational life for any length of time, you've likely seen dozens of examples of poor managerial leadership that were rooted in personal insecurity.

So, as you move into the executive level, the first challenge is to keep insecurity from getting the better of you. Unless you are super-human, your first days as an executive will naturally produce some uncertainty and discomfort. You have moved out of a series of roles that have become more and more familiar and in which you have been able to regularly demonstrate your competence and ability to get things done. After all, if you hadn't been doing that, then you most likely would not have been promoted to the executive team. But, now you're in a new role at a new level with new expectations. You *should* be uncomfortable. If you're not, you are probably under-estimating what's ahead of you.

In spite of this new reality, it is critical for your success that you not dwell on thoughts and self-assessments that cause you to doubt your capacity to contribute as an executive. Rather, you must build a sense of *grounded confidence* in your presence and in the idea that you have important contributions to make as one of the leaders of your organization. In this chapter, some of our executive mentors share their experience and advice about what it takes to operate with grounded confidence at the top levels of an organization. We'll cover mind-sets and behaviors that, if consistently applied, will help you pick up confidence in your presence as an executive and let go of doubt in how you contribute.

## From the Tactical to the Transformational

Before we get to the advice, let's talk a bit about methods and tactics. Regularly demonstrating your confidence in a grounded and appropriate way will build the confidence of your boss, your peers, and your team in you. As someone in a new, highly visible, and high-stakes role, showing up with confidence right out of the gate might seem like a tall order. Doing so will require some intention and awareness on your part about how you want to appear to others and yourself—along with a willingness to do some things that rein-force your intention and likelihood of success. Building your confi-dence in your executive role can begin with some tactics that, when you make them part of your routine, can lead to transformational changes that dramatically raise your level of leadership effectiveness.

Aristotle said, "We are what we repeatedly do. Excellence, then, is not an act but a habit." While it might feel overly tactical and even a bit artificial to identify a few behaviors to do repeatedly, taking this approach is, as Aristotle declared, the path to excellence. As an exec-utive coach, I help my clients identify the result they want to achieve and then assess what behaviors and mind-sets they need to adopt to achieve those results. That is the premise of this book. As you reach the executive level, there are some behaviors and mind-sets you'll want to keep. In all likelihood, your capacity to show up with grounded confidence will flow from a number of your keeper behav-iors. It is equally likely, though, that you will need to both pick up and let go of some other behaviors and mind-sets in order to come across with the confidence and presence that will lead your new peers to accept you fully as a member of the executive team. The opportunity you have is to identify the key tactical behaviors that, if regularly repeated, will lead to a transformation in the level of con-fidence you project with your fellow executives and in the organiza-tion as a whole.

In this chapter, our executive mentors will identify a number of important factors in growing into an executive presence that projects grounded confidence. As you consider their perspectives, I encourage you to conduct some self-assessment and reflection on which of the identified characteristics you already possess and which you will need to pick up and let go of. To take your assessment process further and make it more powerful, use the colleague feedback process presented in Appendix A as the Executive Success Plan™ (ESP™) to get advice on what you should keep doing, start doing, and stop doing to show up with a confident executive presence. The ESP also outlines a straightforward process for following up on feedback in a way that will move you from tactical execution to transformative results.

## Results and Relationships

Whether you have already reached the executive level or are fast approaching it, your focus on achieving results has almost certainly been one of the primary reasons for your success. What may not be as certain is whether you have managed relationships as successfully as you have achieved results. As a star individual contributor or a high-powered functional team leader, you may well have been able to achieve results through force of will and dogged persistence. In such cases, relationships are sometimes not as important as getting the result. As an executive, you will find that this is no longer the case. To achieve and sustain results over the long run at the executive level, strong relationships with peers, top leadership, and functional team members across the organization are critical.

Your success in managing relationships will stem from the confidence you have in yourself and your ability to work well with others to make things happen. Effective relationship management comes from regularly demonstrating the behaviors that you engage in when you're operating at your best. For most of us, we know we're operating at our best when we feel comfortable, engaged, and effective. When we feel that way, we feel confident. Jason Jeffay, partner with the management consulting firm Hewitt Associates, has this advice for new executives about personal confidence and its impact on building strong relationships that support results:

Know that you are where you are . . . because you should be in that role. So you neither have to formally prove yourself nor be intimidated. If you go too far in proving yourself, you are probably going to turn people off. If, on the other hand, you are clearly intimidated by now being in this position and don't contribute anything to those peer-to-peer relationships, people will discount you and say, "Yeah, you probably don't belong in the role." So navigate [between] those two rocks as you head down the stream and that's where you want to be.

## Work from How You Are at Your Best

Leaders who navigate between the rocks and project genuine confidence that inspires the trust and appreciation of others begin with a clear understanding and acknowledgment of the characteristics they demonstrate when they are at their best. Each of us is unique in the mix of perspective and personality we bring to the leadership table. Being a successful executive does not require you to change who you are, but it may require you to change what you regularly do so that you are more likely to be operating from the state of how you are at your best.

Donna Morea is president of CGI-AMS, a computer systems consulting company headquartered in Fairfax, Virginia. Donna was a manager and executive for more than twenty years in the predecessor company, American Management Systems (AMS), until it was acquired by the Canadian firm CGI in 2004. With the integration of the two companies, Donna was appointed president of the U.S. division. Donna shares what she has learned over the course of her career about the confidence and effectiveness that comes from operating from how you are when you're at your best:

For me, I have found that as I become more confident in my role as an executive, I'm actually a lot more "me" today than I was twenty years ago. I know how to channel it in a way. I'm a little bit unorthodox . . . but I figured out how to make it work. I really do believe that it is important for you to be you. Figuring out how to bring together the demands of the [role] as well as how you are is the art of this whole thing.

I don't believe that you should ever be anything other than who you are. I'm a little more social than the [typical executive]. I'm a little more personally intimate and friendly. For many years, I thought I had to shut that out. I have had some good friends and coaches who have helped me see that being who you are really makes it a lot easier to come to work every day. It's about figuring out a way to channel that in alignment with the role. I wish I had discovered that a little bit earlier. It sure would have been a lot more fun.

Donna has developed a confident executive presence by understanding how she is when she's operating at her best and allowing that person to come through. Donna's strategy will work for you, but her specific approach to leadership won't. Your approach will be different based on how you are when you're at your best. It will reflect *your* unique personality and preferences for how to spend your time, organize your life, solve problems, make decisions, and interact with others. The key to operating with confidence at your best is to understand your natural makeup and leverage your preferences. To learn more about how you are when you are at your best, I recommend that you work with a coach who is experienced in administering and interpreting one or more of the reputable and well-researched style and personality inventories that are available on the market.

## Get Comfortable with Letting Go of What Brought You to the Dance

In talking about what it takes to project a confident presence, Bob Johnson, senior vice president of operations for Nextel, says, "You probably have to change what you do, but not who you are. That is very important because as a leader you have to be true to yourself and act with conviction regardless of the situation. . . . It is very transparent and fake if you come to work and become somebody different all of a sudden."

There are two important points to note about what Johnson said:

*First, don't change who you are.* Johnson is a successful executive because he is focused, driven to achieve results, and willing to learn and adjust to achieve those results. That's how he is when he's operating at his best. His at-his-best profile is different from Donna Morea's but it works for him and his colleagues just as hers does for her. They both project confidence by understanding how they are at their best and demonstrating those qualities consistently.

*Second, you probably have to change what you do.* Note that changing what you do is a completely different thing from changing how you are when you are at your best. We have already talked about how confidence flows from a state of being comfortable and engaged. Becoming an executive will challenge and stretch you to move beyond your existing comfort level. In all likelihood, one of the things that makes you comfortable is acting on the technical or functional knowledge that you have developed throughout your career. What brought you to the dance, what got you to the executive level, is probably your proven ability in a particular functional skill set. To succeed at the executive level, you will, as Bob Johnson suggests, have to change what you do. The old adage—"Dance with the one that brung ya"—is not true when it comes to executives and their technical expertise. If you continue to dance with your technical expertise, you will not have the time or perspective to live up to the new expectations of you as an executive leader of your organization.

To meet the expectations that your peers and top management have of you, you will have to let go of deep engagement in the day-to-day aspects of your function. Because that level of engagement has become familiar and comfortable, letting go of it can shake your confidence. As Jason Jeffay observes, "Most people have more ability than confidence."

At forty-three, Sid Fuchs is one of the youngest division presidents at defense contractor Northrop Grumman Corporation (NGC). Before becoming president of NGC's TASC business unit, Fuchs had a career that spanned both the technical and the marketing aspects of his industry. In his interview for this book, he talked about the process of letting go that an executive has to undergo to be successful at the next level:

> One of the big transition points in my life was realizing that I had to give up something, to let go of the need to feel like I was the expert. When I was coming up through the ranks as an engineer, I was a pretty good engineer. . . . I was up to speed on the current technologies and . . . was always looked upon as the expert in my area.
>
> As I worked in different companies and moved up, I realized I was spending more time doing the technology piece and that I wasn't spending enough time developing the leadership skills I needed to lead people or lead an organization. And so I had to make a very conscious decision that I was not going to be an engineer anymore.
>
> I think in those kinds of situations people feel that they are giving up something. But, when a door closes another one opens, right? I believe that most people don't view it as I have to close this door to open another. It requires learning all over again and some people don't want to have to learn all over again.

It is hard to let go of what has made you successful and learn the new skills needed to succeed at the next level. Bill Plamondon, former CEO of Budget Rent A Car, believes that people tend to feel insecure when they begin something new: "Whether it's a position or a new company or new level, people tend to go back to what allowed them or allows them to be comfortable."

Mark Stavish, former senior vice president of human resources for America Online, shares a similar thought: "When we are thrown into difficult situations, we tend to resort to things that were successful for us." The pull of the comfortable is very powerful, but it can be very damaging. To develop the confidence needed to succeed as an executive, you will have to explore fields beyond the comfort of the functional skills that brought you to the dance. If you continue to draw your confidence from the skills and knowledge that brought you to the next level, you will probably not stay there very long; your vision and capacity to make a broader impact will be too narrow and limited.

## Pick Up the Confidence
## That You Can Do It Differently

As an executive, you are now expected to contribute to defining opportunities and solving problems for the organization as a whole, not just within your functional area of expertise. To play this broader leadership role, you will have to develop and project a sense of confidence in your judgment that extends beyond functional or technical knowledge. Having the confidence to take a learning stance in your new role will help you get there much more quickly. Do your homework before meetings with fellow executives. Don't be afraid to ask questions.

Joni Reich is senior vice president of administration for Sallie Mae, a leader in the student loan industry and one of the largest financial institutions in the United States. Reich has spent most of her career at Sallie Mae, coming up through the ranks in different human resources roles before assuming her current job. She offers this perspective on how taking a learning stance helped her to build the confidence to learn and contribute at the executive level:

> I was a little bit of a fish out of water in the sense that until you have an opportunity to really work with a CEO or a chief

operating officer and to be in the room when they are running the company week to week, you can't really prepare for that. You don't really know what that is like until you are there. . . . I had always dealt with HR people or I dealt with division heads. Well, obviously, they have a lot that they need to get done and . . . that they are facing every day. But I had never really been at the top level until I was there and so I had to learn very quickly. Mostly it was about listening first, of course, to learn what was going on, what needed to get done, and then doing it. That's what our CEO describes when he talks to our young managers about leadership. The way he likes to short-hand it is to say that we are both thinkers and doers with an equal emphasis on both roles. We are thinkers in the sense of [being clear] about what we are talking about. We need to be people [who] get it and who can be astute about seeing where our business is and where we are evolving. What are the imped-iments or the challenges that we face, and how does our role fit into the big picture? And then we are doers, in terms of people who make it happen, people who advance the ball on a day-to-day basis and are constructive rather than conversationalists.

The CEO that Joni referred to was Al Lord. Over the past ten years, Lord, his successor, Tim Fitzpatrick, and their team have cre-ated significant amounts of additional value for Sallie Mae's share-holders and customers. As CEO, Lord expected his executive team to learn, think clearly, and act.

Taking constructive action that moves the organization forward will be a key aspect of how you are assessed as an executive. Obviously, it takes confidence to take action when you don't know everything you would like to know about a situation or when you have the feeling that your level of knowledge is not what it was when you were a functional leader. My advice as a coach is to get used to it. At the executive level, you are playing on a bigger and broader field but with less information and control than you had as a functional leader. In partnership with your colleagues, you have to learn what you can, ask good questions that draw out the information needed to make a decision, and then act. Most of the time, you won't have all the information you'd like to have. You still have to act. Making those tough decisions is, as they say, why you're getting paid the big bucks.

A few months ago, I had a great conversation with Mike Lanier, director of marketing for Verizon. In his entry-level executive position, Mike regularly works with vice presidents and senior vice presidents in an intensely competitive industry, so the pace is fast and demanding. Mike and I spent a good part of our time talking about the impact that having confidence has on executive decision making and execution. Let me share part of our discussion:

SCOTT: Mike, were you basically convinced that you belonged at this level when you were appointed director?

MIKE: Yeah, I was.

SCOTT: One of the things I find is that sometimes people aren't. They are a little tentative when they are promoted. Do you ever see that with your peers—that they maybe don't lead as much as they should?

MIKE: I do, you know, and that is a good point because I think that is the separation between the ones who are more successful and the ones who aren't. I had some coaching one time early on in my career, which was, "Don't think about failure or what you might not be able to do. Just focus on how you are going to get it done."

SCOTT: It sounds like the advice to a tightrope walker, "Don't look down."

MIKE: Yeah. I was just in a meeting where we were talking about this. If you think you can or if you think you can't, you will. It's like *Apollo 13*, failure is not an option. If you think about that, you have to say, "OK, just come up with a game plan and focus on it."

SCOTT: Yeah. That's a great point. So, I guess it's the opposite of the deer in the headlights thing, right?

MIKE: Yeah. You see that occasionally, but that usually doesn't last very long because you stick out like a sore thumb.

I want to be clear about the type of action Mike and I were talking about when he said, "Just focus on how you're going to get it done." In Chapter 7, I'll talk at greater length about how successful executives drive outcomes. In the context of this discussion about picking up the confidence needed to contribute as an executive, it is important to say that you will need to get comfortable with having a different mind-set about what makes you feel like you have accomplished something at the end of the day. When you're operating as an executive, your accomplishments will be more about influencing outcomes than directly creating outcomes. Remember, you will have to let go of your comfort and confidence coming from knowing and acting on your functional expertise. If you go there, you will be playing below the level at which you are expected to play as an executive. Your daily sense of accomplishment and having made a contribution can no longer be about what *you* accomplished today. It has to be about what you led, influenced, or coached others to accomplish. That being said, let's look in some depth at four other tactics that, if practiced regularly, can have a transformative effect on your executive presence:

- View yourself as a peer
- Silence your inner critic
- Visualize how you want to show up
- Trust your gut

## View Yourself as a Peer

When you are promoted to the executive level you are likely to feel as though people are treating you differently. If that's the case, there is a reason for it: They *are* treating you differently. I'll address this phenomenon more later in Chapter 10, on picking up a big-footprint view of your role. For the purposes of this discussion of confidence, I want to specifically speak to the issue of how your executive peers view you. In most organizations, the process of becoming an executive is rigorous and is somewhat reminiscent of the sort of natural selection Darwin described. If you have gotten to this level, you have in all likelihood been deemed by the people already there to be one of the fittest and strongest. Your new executive peers are selective in who they invite to join their club. Having said they want you on their team, they expect you to know how to play. Steve Linehan, senior vice president and treasurer of Capital One, sums up the executive selection process like this: "Once you are through, we all know you are good. And, the fact is, our expectation is that you contribute at the table, whatever table you are sitting around."

Note Linehan's words well: "Our expectation is that you contribute at the table." You are now a peer of the other executives. You are expected to contribute. It is, however, important that you contribute in a way that your peers appreciate. How you do that will depend on the cultural norms of your organization.

Lucien Alziari, as senior vice president of human resources for Avon Corporation and a former senior HR leader for PepsiCo, has worked successfully in two very different cultures. The Pepsi culture has historically been hard charging and one in which you are expected to make your mark early and often. The culture at Avon values collaboration and, Alziari says, places a premium on executives' acting with emotional intelligence. In comparing the strategies of how new executives in the two companies successfully establish themselves as peers of their colleagues, Alziari had this to say:

> At PepsiCo, it was really important that you got out of the gate quickly. That within a short period of time you had at least an initial view on what the agenda would be and that you had the self-confidence to engage fully as a vice president on the business team. I used to tell people there that the best way of

becoming a vice president was to behave like a vice president when you were a director. So, I used to say, embarrass us into doing the right thing. But the other benefit of that is when you actually get into the role, it is not such a huge transition because if you have done it well you will feel like it's just part of a continuum that you have already been on. It isn't such a big change.

At Avon, there is some of that same level of expectation but there is much more of a premium on humility in Avon's culture. So, in some ways you have to be a lot more measured about how you get out of the gate and not come across as knowing the answers before you ask the right questions. That may be more of a function of coming in new to the company but I suspect it is also true as you move into the leadership teams here that there is more of a premium on making sure you understand it before you tell us we should change it.

I think my [general] advice would be . . . to have an agenda but make sure you understand what it is that you are talking about. In both companies, I advise executives to be *in* the family before you comment *on* the family.

Earlier in this chapter, I used the term *grounded confidence*. When Lucien Alziari offers the advice "to have an agenda, but make sure you understand what it is that you are talking about," he is encouraging you to show up with grounded confidence. Once you're an executive, your peers are looking to you to be a thought leader who is focused on where the organization needs to go. They don't expect you to show up as a junior person who is not adding value to the conversation and decision-making process.

In my first few senior staff meetings as an executive, I was so nervous that my mouth was dry and it was hard to speak. After a few weeks, I realized that I knew enough about what was going on and had a point of view that could add to the quality of the conversation. Create opportunities for yourself to establish familiarity and rapport with your peers outside regular executive group meetings. Doing this will help build your confidence and get you past the intimidation factor that comes from being the new kid on the block. Alexander Caillet, a coach I know, likes to say that presence begets presence. If you project discomfort or insecurity, your peers will sense it and become uncomfortable with you and your judgment. Likewise, if you project a confident and comfortable presence, your peers will sense that and will return the favor.

## Silence Your Inner Critic

Most of us, no matter how successful we've been, occasionally hear a little mental voice that offers "helpful" advice: "There's a lot riding on this presentation, so don't mess it up," or "The last time you faced this situation, you really blew it. Don't let it happen again." You've likely heard this voice referred to as your "inner critic." I've also heard it called the "itty bitty shitty committee." Whatever you call it, it's important to recognize when it's speaking and tell it to give it a rest. Without going too deep into psychology, I can assure you that your inner critic is trying to protect you from failure or harm. Ironically, in telling you what not to do or what you should do to avoid failure, your itty bitty committee is keeping you from performing from the stance of how you are at your best. Tennis and executive coach Tim Gallwey sums up this phenomenon well in his book *The Inner Game of Work.* Gallwey has come up with a descriptive equation for the phenomenon:

$$P = p - i$$

Gallwey's equation means *Performance is equal to potential minus interference.* Based on his wide-ranging coaching experience, he makes the point that performance rarely equals potential because we create interference for ourselves that detracts from the potential. That interference shows up as those helpful, fear-based instructions intended to ward off failure or embarrassment.

About ten years ago, I had the opportunity to take a short tennis lesson from Tim Gallwey as part of an executive development course at the University of Southern California. After sharing some of his concepts with us in the classroom, Tim announced that we were going to head outside to the tennis courts and asked for three volunteers: a tennis novice, an intermediate player, and someone who felt like an advanced player. Having only swatted a tennis ball around a few times before in my life, I volunteered to be the novice.

As the thirty of us went outside to the tennis courts, I started wondering why I had volunteered. My sport is running, which is wonderful for me because it doesn't require a lot of hand-eye coordination—something I don't exactly possess in buckets. As Tim called me up to the baseline, I started thinking that this was probably going to be a bit embarrassing. He gave me a racket and a ball and then proceeded to position my hands on the racket, get my feet pointed in the right direction and the appropriate distance apart, my head angled just so, turned my upper torso in the right direction, and then shouted, "OK, hit the ball!" That was his example for the group of how not to teach or coach. In giving me so many things to think about, Gallwey was purposely adding to the interference I already had going on about not embarrassing myself in front of the group.

Tim then said, "What I'm going to do is go to the other side of the net and toss some balls to you. We're not going to play tennis, we're going to play a game called bounce-hit. Scott, when you see the ball bounce, I want you to say 'bounce.' If it bounces twice, say 'bounce' twice. If it bounces once, say 'bounce' once, and so on. When you hit the ball with the racket, I want you to say 'hit.'"

So we started playing bounce-hit and that was easy: "Bounce, bounce, hit. Bounce, hit. Bounce, bounce, bounce, hit."

"Now," Tim said, "I'm going to start lobbing them to you with my racket instead of my hand. We're not playing tennis yet, we're still playing bounce-hit."

It was still pretty easy for me: "Bounce, bounce, hit. Bounce, hit. Bounce, hit."

"OK, it seems like you're getting this," Tim said. "I'm going to pick up the pace a little bit. We're still playing bounce-hit."

This was actually fun. "Bounce, hit," I said after running to the right to stroke the ball. "Bounce-hit," as I ran back to the left to return it with a backhand. We went on this way for four or five minutes before I realized that I was no longer saying "bounce, hit"—and before I realized that I had not missed a shot. I was volleying with Tim Gallwey, having fun, receiving the applause of my classmates, and just working from my potential without the interference.

One way to think about interference is that it is whatever keeps you from performing in the position of how you are when you're at your best. It can show up as negative self-talk, ungrounded fear, or stories that you have about what others are doing or thinking. As an example, watch out for creating interference for yourself by expecting much coaching or affirmation from your executive-level peers or superiors. It's nice when you get it, but don't expect it and don't worry about why you're not getting it if you're not. At the executive level, most people are so consumed with their own agendas that they are not left with a lot of peripheral vision to notice what others are doing. Ed Sannini, a managing director of Morgan Stanley, has noticed that becoming an executive means that "you get to a point where your management is no longer going to spend a lot of time coaching you. You don't go to them asking, 'What should I do?' You make the decision and communicate the decision versus looking for affirmation."

The more successful senior executives differentiate themselves by noticing what others are doing and then coaching or applauding as appropriate. That is one of the things that sets them apart and that can set you apart over the longer run. In the meantime, don't create a lot of needless interference with your performance if you're not getting much stroking. In all likelihood, it's not all about you.

## Visualize How You Want to Show Up

Golfers are familiar with the concept of developing a "positive swing thought." Before swinging the club and hitting the ball, an accomplished golfer will visualize the desired result and the swing it will take to produce that result. While the result doesn't always match up to the thought, a positive swing thought is much more likely to yield a good outcome than a negative swing thought or no particular thought at all. In coaching my executive clients, particularly the ones who play golf, I encourage them to use the concept of the positive swing thought before meetings or important conversations. I want them to ask themselves, "What do I want to accomplish in this meeting?" and "How do I need to show up to accomplish that?"

It's hard to imagine a meeting in which a positive outcome would not be served by showing up with the confidence that flows from how you are at your best. Over the years, I've coached both extroverted and introverted clients. Based on your observations, you've probably noticed that it appears easier for extroverts to participate (and sometimes dominate) in meetings. Business culture, especially in the United States, puts a premium on speaking up. It's one of the litmus tests (when not overdone) for assessing whether someone has the confidence and wherewithal to make a contribution. While extroverts should monitor themselves to make sure they're not talking too much, introverts usually need to develop strategies to be sure they contribute enough.

When coaching introverted clients, I often receive feedback from their colleagues that they need to speak up more in meetings. When I talk with my clients about this, I encourage them to notice in the next meeting they go to how often someone says something accepted by the group as brilliant that is something my client has been thinking but has not said. They usually find that this occurs fairly frequently. Introverts need time to process their thoughts before sharing them with others. To help them learn to share their thoughts more quickly in meetings, I encourage my clients to try a number of things. First, I ask them to practice their swing thought before the meeting by asking themselves questions like these:

- What is this meeting going to be about?

- What is my point of view on that subject?

- What outcome do I want from the meeting?

- What ideas will I need to share to reach that outcome?

- What are the top two or three points I want to make?

- How do I want to make them?

By doing this sort of preparation, introverts can more comfortably participate in the give-and-take of a conversation and demonstrate confidence through their participation. This is also not a bad routine for extroverts to go through as well, as it can help them boil down their points to the most important and keep them from running on longer than is necessary or effective.

## Trust Your Gut

Perhaps the ultimate test of confidence in the executive setting is when the crowd is moving in one direction and your gut instinct tells you it's the wrong way. It could be that a poor business decision is being made or, as recent events in the business world have shown, it could be a poor ethical decision. I've had a number of executives tell me the importance of learning to listen to and rely on their instincts. As one of them said to me, "If it smells bad, you're probably right."

Looking back on my experience as an executive, this makes sense to me. Particularly when I was new to an executive team, I sometimes heard positions advocated that just didn't seem to make sense. At the time, I told myself that because I'm new I just must not understand. But I was wrong. It was the new perspective I brought that caused my instincts to alert me to things that didn't make sense. As a new member of the executive team, you can sometimes see things that the people who have been on the team a while may no longer see. It takes confidence—and sometimes courage—to speak up and share your point of view on actions that you think could lead to a train wreck.

I am not suggesting that you have to always share your opinion in the group. It may be more appropriate and effective to share your concerns outside the group and check out your perceptions or influence your peers in one-to-one conversations. Another alternative is to suggest to the team that an external perspective be sought before proceeding. As one executive said to me, "When everyone in the room is absolutely certain about what needs to be done, that's the signal to say, "Wait a minute, have we looked at this from every angle and heard from everyone on this?""

It takes confidence to speak up, and to do a lot of the other things we've discussed in this chapter. Developing grounded confidence is the foundation of being an effective executive leader. It is worth the effort to identify and regularly pursue the tactics that will lead you to pick up the transformative confidence that you can contribute at the next level.

**10 TIPS**  **For Picking Up Confidence in Your Presence and Letting Go of Doubt in How You Contribute**

1  Build awareness of how you are at your best through coaching based on objective assessment, colleague feedback, and self-observation.

2  Get comfortable with changing what you do by letting go of the need to feel like a functional expert.

3  Take a learning stance to better understand the issues at the executive level and how you can make a contribution.

4  Be prepared to act without having all the information you might like to have.

5  Reframe your definition of what your daily contribution to the result should be: It should be about influencing others to create the result, not creating the result yourself.

6  Act as a peer consistent with the cultural norms of your organization and executive team.

7  Prepare yourself to share points of view that add quality to the executive conversation and decision-making process.

8  Identify the interference that keeps you from performing at your best and minimize it.

9  Develop a routine of visualizing the desired outcome and how you need to show up to get it.

10  Trust your gut and speak up when you believe a poor decision is about to be made.

# 3

# PICK UP REGULAR RENEWAL OF YOUR ENERGY AND PERSPECTIVE

# LET GO OF RUNNING FLAT OUT UNTIL YOU CRASH

When faced with a challenge, a natural response for many leaders is to bear down and speed up. Having chalked up success after success, they see each new challenge as simply another hurdle to jump over. They believe that all it should take is more of what brought them to that point: smarts and a willingness to work harder and do more than the competition. The problem with this approach at the executive level is that it is one new challenge after another.

If your immediate response in the face of every new challenge is to bear down and speed up, you will eventually run out of gas and crash. As Martin Carter, president of Hydro Aluminum North America, told me, "As an executive, there is a huge onslaught on your time and your energy. Everybody seems to want a piece of you and managing that is very critical." Managing the demands of executive life requires picking up regular renewal of your energy and perspective and letting go of running flat out until you crash. For someone who has reached the heights of the organization by working harder and longer than the next guy, letting go of running flat out can feel like a leap of faith. The thought is, If I don't keep running, I'm going to fall behind; I can't stop. This kind of thinking is more or less the antithesis of performing with a sense of grounded confidence in your capacity to contribute as an executive. The transformative challenge for new executives is to learn to take the regular breaks needed to renew the energy and perspective that enable them to perform at their best.

## Exertion, Then Recovery

In *The Power of Full Engagement,* authors Jim Loehr and Tony Schwartz draw a comparison between marathoners and sprinters. They note that many people believe that life is a marathon, not a sprint. But, how many of us, they ask, really want to be marathoners? What's the difference between the two? The standard training regimen for marathoners is to run continuously over miles and miles. Sprinters train through a cycle of exertion and recovery. They sprint for two hundred meters and walk for two hundred meters and then sprint for two hundred meters and walk for two hundred more. Having worked with both professional athletes and professional executives, Loehr and Schwartz argue that both groups should approach their work in the same way, with a cycle of exertion and recovery.

Even brief periods of recovery or downtime can make a huge difference in executive performance. Over the years, I've coached a number of clients who worked seven days a week, clocking ten or eleven hours a day Monday through Friday and then putting in at least three or four hours each on Saturday and Sunday. The upshot of this approach to work is invariably a feeling of always being behind and, not surprisingly, burned out from never getting a break.

When I work with clients in this mode, I always ask them to run an experiment for me. My request is that they pick one day of the upcoming weekend to not do any work, no matter how behind they believe they are. I encourage them to pick Sunday over Saturday because I want them to have at least twenty-four hours away from their to-do list immediately before heading to the office on Monday morning. After they take a weekend day off, I call or e-mail them late in the day on Monday or early on Tuesday with this question, "How was your Monday?" The answer is almost always the same: "Better than usual."

My clients find that they think more clearly, interact more easily with others, and are more relaxed after just one day away from thinking about work. For most of them (and maybe for you as well), the thought of taking a day for themselves to sleep late, hang out with their friends or family, see a movie, play a game, or even run some errands is alluring and frightening at the same time. For executives who already feel the pressure to get through yet more work, stepping off the treadmill of working seven days a week seems like a leap of faith. But, breaking the cycle of continuous exertion allows some time for recovery and reconnection to how they are at their best.

## Perspective and Peak Performance

When I talk about connecting to how you are at your best, I am asking you to think about how you perform and feel when you are at your most confident and relaxed. Athletes call this state being in the zone. Psychologist Mihaly Csikszentmihalyi calls it *flow*. Whatever you call it, it is when your level of engagement is in that sweet spot between apathy and brain-lock-inducing stress. Operating at this level of engagement creates the opportunity to perform at the peak of your capabilities and potential. To do that requires developing routines that enable you to recharge your energy stores and regain perspective.

One of the metaphors I like to use to describe this process comes from Ron Heifetz, who believes that leaders need to regularly "get up on the balcony." His point—which I previewed in Chapter 1—is that, as a leader, it is too easy to be down on the dance floor where all you can see is your partner and maybe a few of the dancers around you. When you take the time to leave the dance floor and get up on the balcony, you get a perspective on everything that is going on. You can see the patterns that sweep across the floor. You can see who is dancing well and who is struggling. You can even see that maybe you need to stop dancing with the one who brought you! After you gain that perspective, you can return to the floor and apply your attention where it is needed the most.

When I first arrived at Columbia Gas Transmission as VP of human resources, I quickly got myself into a state of feeling overwhelmed with all the things that appeared to need my attention. My response was to dance faster—to take on more and more meetings —rather than get up on the balcony and look at what were really the best things for me to be involved in. Cathy Abbott, my boss and the CEO of the company, recognized this in me and, during my first year, would regularly remind me that she needed me to stay sane and not go crazy by trying to attend to too many things at once. Almost ten years later, it was a real pleasure to interview her for this book and revisit her thinking on the importance of perspective. Like a number of the other executives who shared their thoughts on moving to the next level, Cathy Abbott talked about the shift in comfort level and approach that is required to be fully effective as an executive:

> As you move into the executive ranks, a lot of your value is in having the capacity to handle the unexpected garbage that

lands on your desk because it has not gotten resolved. And in order to do that you can't be so overworked and frustrated and close to the edge that you don't have that kind of dispassionate ability to look at the situation through somewhat different eyes. I think a big risk is that the habits of working hard and pushing yourself that may have served you extremely well up to this point can become a disadvantage because you lose that perspective that you are paid to have as an executive. If you have yourself so scheduled up, or you are always on the road or always in meetings, you can't manage those unexpected things. In that state of overload, if you do try to manage the unexpected problem, you may turn it into more of a crisis than it needs to be rather than solving it.

## Choosing to Perform at Your Best

Operating at peak performance demands that you make a choice to establish the routines that enable you to perform at your best. As an executive, you will face a lot of pressure to react to dozens of demands on multiple fronts at any given time. You will undoubtedly be charged with leading change as the marketplace and your organization evolve. Because change almost always involves loss as well as gain, you will run into resistance, lack of understanding, anger, and other responses that can make life difficult and uncomfortable.

You can choose to react to these demands by taking on more and more meetings, answering e-mail at home every evening, skipping lunch, ignoring your health and key relationships, and basically running flat out until you crash. Alternatively, you can choose to respond to the demands by intentionally establishing routines designed to help you perform at your best.

Tough times are guaranteed when you're an executive. When times get tough, either you can rely on the foundation you've established through routines of renewal or you can just react to what's in front of you. Obviously, the smart choice is to take the time to establish and practice the routines that bring out the best in you. This is the basis for making the smart strategic choices that I talked about in the Preface. Operating from that approach will support you in performing at your peak not just at work but in your life at home and in the broader community as well. In times of change and uncertainty, understanding and acting on how you are when you are at your best is the foundation of peak performance. Taking the steps needed to make that the basis for consistently performing at your peak can give you the confidence and capacity needed to navigate the uncharted terrain that is in front of you as an executive.

## Navigating Uncharted Terrain with Your Life GPS®

Several years ago, my wife and I developed a tool for helping ourselves identify how each of us is at our best, what we need to regularly do to support performing at our best and connecting that performance to key goals in the different arenas of our life. Diane and I have trademarked that tool as the Life Goals Planning System, or Life GPS® for short.

Over the past ten years, the Global Positioning System has become an increasingly familiar part of everyday life. With a GPS receiver, you can determine your exact location on a hike in the woods, in your car, or standing on a city street corner. Knowing exactly where you are makes it much easier to determine where you want to go and how to get there. Most people would like to have the same sense of clarity in their personal and professional lives.

My clients have found that using the Life GPS process enables them to capture on one sheet of paper what is most important in their life, what they need to consistently do to serve what is most important, and the means to remind them of how they are at their best. Based on my experience and that of my clients, I believe that taking time to create and regularly review your Life GPS is an important step in learning to pick up the habit of renewing the energy and perspective that will help you be an effective executive. In the next few pages, I will help you create your Life GPS. I encourage you to read through the process and then, over the next few days, set aside an hour or two to think through the different elements of your Life GPS.

## How Are You at Your Best?

Creating your Life GPS begins with identifying the core characteristics that describe how you are when you are at your best. To identify the characteristics that are central to you, think of situations you've been in when you are most relaxed, productive, effective, or energized. Get some clear pictures of those situations in your mind. What are the four or five words or short phrases that describe you in your best state? Be careful to avoid words that describe how you think you should be or how you'd like to be. We are each wired differently. The characteristics that describe best-state performance for one executive will be entirely different for the next. Choose the words or phrases that describe how *you* are at your best. Solely for purposes of providing an example, the words that describe me at my best are *learning, being a catalyst, guiding, excelling,* and *connecting.* Those are the words that describe me when I am functioning at my best as a husband, parent, coach, friend, or any other role I fill in my life. What are the words or key ideas that describe how you are at your best? Write them down in the center of a piece of paper.

## What Should You Repeatedly Do?

In Chapter 2 I shared the quote from Aristotle that says, "We are what we repeatedly do. Excellence, then, is not an act but a habit." The next step in creating your Life GPS is to identify a short list of routine actions in four key domains of experience that—if you did them regularly—would reinforce how you are at your best. Those domains are the mental, physical, spiritual, and relational. The characteristics that describe you at your best will lead to a short list of actions for you to repeatedly do in each domain. When you stop and think about it, the importance of regularly taking positive action in these four domains is intuitive. A Fortune 500 vice president told me what happened to him by not following this practice during a particularly stressful period in his career:

> Things at work got more and more crazy and I stopped investing in myself. I should have done the exact opposite. I should have invested more in myself physically, mentally, personally, and professionally. The situation at work was so overwhelming, though, and felt like such a big thing, that I kept focusing on just that. I lost sight of the bigger picture. I needed to keep investing in all those other things that are the makeup of who I am. Instead, I was getting caught up in the crap.

> You have to make sure that you are continually tuning yourself. I mean how many footballs do you think Tom Brady throws a day? He didn't stop throwing a bunch of footballs every day because he and the Patriots won a couple of Super Bowls. He probably throws twice as many. I didn't do that when things got crazy. I screwed up. I made a mistake. You continually have to hone your craft and I stopped investing in me. My wife was the one who pointed it out to me. Nobody on the business side said anything, but, boy, did it have professional ramifications for me.

> Things at work improved once I went back to taking care of the complete picture. I'm back to working out. I don't miss church. I make sure that I dedicate the time to my family. Those are some of the routines that brought me here and I've found that as I move up they almost become more critical and more important to my success. When pieces of your foundation start falling away there is a pretty quick domino effect. I have

watched it happen with several senior executives that are no longer with this company.

By returning to the routines that provide him with a sense of how he is when he's at his best, this executive has built a foundation that supports him in keeping his perspective intact and his performance high when the terrain gets rough.

## Establishing Reinforcing Routines

Let's take a brief look at the four domains of experience in which you'll want to establish routines of renewal. I'm not going to go into great detail on each domain because what matters most is that you identify routines that will help create the conditions for *you* to perform at *your* best. Again, as an example, to reinforce my core characteristic of connecting, my routine in the mental domain is to journal regularly about the quality of the relationships that are most important to me and to reflect on what I can do to sustain and strengthen them. My routines in the physical domain are centered on eating well, staying in shape, and taking care of my appearance so I have the energy and self-confidence I need to want to connect with people. In the spiritual domain, to reinforce the characteristic of connecting, I have established a routine of serving people in the community who need help. In the relational domain, I make it a point to look for opportunities to connect by doing interesting work with interesting people. These routines and others I've established not only reinforce connection for me but also support the characteristics of learning, guiding, excelling, and being a catalyst that represent how I am when I am at my best. Obviously, the process of identifying routines that reinforce your core characteristics is more art than science. You will learn by trial and error the routines that work best to create the conditions for you to perform at your best. The point is not to create the perfect list but to increase self-awareness of what works for you and to be more intentional about doing what it takes to operate at peak performance. With that said, here are a few thought starters on how to develop routines in each of the four domains of life experience.

## Mental

No pun intended, but when you think about it, absolutely everything anyone does starts with a thought. Because the quality of the thought has a large influence on the quality of the outcome, it makes sense to do what you can to think clearly. In a world in which technology provides the capacity to reach out and be reached anytime, anywhere, finding space to think clearly is more and more of a challenge. A lack of white space on one's calendar correlates with a lack of white space in one's brain. As an executive, you'll find it easy to let your calendar get jammed with appointments to the point where you are moving from one event to the next with very little time to get up on the balcony and see what it all means. My former boss, Cathy Abbott, shared a story and perspective with me that illustrates the downside of this approach:

> I can remember one time talking to another executive who said he was in meetings from morning until night and I asked, "How can you do your job?" and this guy just looked at me. I said, "I see part of my job as leaving enough space to think about what the next issue or problem is that lands on my desk." He just looked at me like I was nuts. It is very counterintuitive, but I think if you leave some white space on your calendar you tend to get more done.

> A full calendar may give the appearance of getting things done, but being able to see that next competitive thing coming down the line or being able to see that we've got two groups that are fighting here and we really need to invest in getting them to work together—those are the critical things that executives

need to do. It is about having that capacity to see further out or to deal with that big threat to your bottom line. The easier issues will get managed below, if you are doing your job right. The higher you are in the organization, the tougher the issues are that come to you. You have to have the space and perspective to deal with those tougher issues. I think a lot of people measure their worth in a corporation by how many meetings they attend. It depends on the culture of the organization you are in, but often it is a huge mistake to fill up your schedule with meetings.

So, if you were going to adjust your routines to allow more time for thinking, what would you spend that time thinking about? Many executives I've worked with have found the value of establishing daily and weekly routines for short-term and long-term planning. Others make time for regular reading inside or outside their business discipline. Bill Gates is well known for taking a week a couple of times each year to retire to a secluded place to read and think across a broad range of topics. An entirely different direction is to use some time to think positively about what's going on in your life and look for ways to reframe negative situations into opportunities. Yet another direction is to develop some routines around being more aware of what is going on in your life. How much of your life do you spend on automatic pilot? As human beings, we tend to sort our routine activities into recurring patterns. This is an unconscious technique we use to keep our brains from being overloaded with thousands of small decisions every day. The risk is that we become so comfortable with our patterns that we extend them to include interactions and decisions requiring attention of their own. However you use the time to strengthen your routines in the mental domain, I encourage you to use it well. A well-known law of computer programming is garbage in, garbage out. Make the opposite true in your mental domain. If you feed your mind good things, good things will result.

## Physical

There has been and will continue to be so much written about how and why to take care of your physical fitness that I see no point in offering many ideas about the subject here. The resources are widely available; I encourage you to use them. I will say, however, a bit about how your physical routines can help reinforce the characteristics of how you are at your best. As noted earlier, the words or ideas that describe you at your best will be unique to you; so, think creatively about how your physical routines can reinforce the characteristics that are uniquely you. For instance, because one of my core characteristics is learning, I regularly look for new things to incorporate into my physical routines. It can be a new workout approach, a new recreational activity, a new item on the menu, or a new travel destination. I look for activities and experiences that satisfy my need to learn new things.

I'm not suggesting that this particular approach would or should work for you. If one of your core characteristics is, for example, consistency, a more regular set of routines in the physical domain would likely work a lot better for you. What I am suggesting is that you draw from the broad array of resources available today to develop a set of physical routines that reinforce how you are at your best. The energy that enables each of us to operate at a level of peak performance begins in our body. It just makes sense to create time to regularly renew it.

## Spiritual

There are many different layers and approaches to the spiritual domain. Without arguing for specific traditions or beliefs, I would suggest that a broadly applicable approach to the spiritual domain comes from Plato, who said that the unexamined life is not worth living. Perhaps the most important form of balcony time that any of us can engage in is to periodically pull up enough to examine the course, quality, and output of our life. I think there is a reason Rick Warren has sold 28 million copies of his book, *The Purpose-Driven Life*. Most of us want to know the answer to the question in his subtitle, What on earth am I here for? Whether you agree or disagree with the content of Warren's book, you can probably identify with the need to define and act on your purpose.

In *Make It Count,* University of Michigan psychologist John Kotre makes the case that most people are driven to do something with their lives that leaves a legacy that matters to the next generation. As you review your list of core characteristics of how you are at your best, I encourage you to identify some routines that draw on those qualities in a way that prepares you to leave the place you're in better than you found it. Obviously, that principle applies to your workplace, but it can certainly extend beyond that arena.

A few years ago, I read an interview in *Harvard Business Review* with Dan Bricklin, the inventor of VisiCalc, the first electronic spreadsheet. In talking about the experiences that shaped his life, Bricklin reflected on the lessons that he had learned in his Jewish day school. He explained that a key principle in Judaism is *tikkun olam.* Tikkun olam is the idea that our job on earth is to take the raw materials we've been given and use them to make something better. For instance, if we're given straw and clay, we can improve on those gifts by using them to make bricks. As you consider what routines to pursue in the spiritual domain, I encourage you to reflect on the combination of the core characteristics that represent how you are at your best. What could you do to really draw them out and make the most of them for the sake of something greater and longer-lasting than yourself?

## Relational

The results-oriented focus of the executive lifestyle can be so all-consuming that it is easy to overlook the relationships inside and outside work that make life richer and more complete. In observing my experience and that of many of my clients, I have found that it is all too easy to focus on short-term results to the detriment of building and sustaining the relationships that make long-term results possible. Apart from the benefits that strong relationships have on achieving results, the mental, physical, and spiritual benefits of establishing positive routines in the relational domain should be enough motivation to pay attention to this area. David Levy, president of the Corcoran Gallery in Washington, D.C., shared a story with me that illustrates how results and relationships need to be kept in balance:

> Earlier in my career when I was leading the Parsons School of Design, I worked on weekends almost all through that period. I would show up at ten in the morning and I would work through four or five in the afternoon in the office, and people started to drift in and work with me. After a while it got to the point where if you called my office on a Saturday or Sunday the secretary would answer the phone. Because I would come in, the secretaries would come in, my other senior staff and some of the junior staff would come in—and they might bring their kids and the kids would be running around doing something and playing around the offices. It wouldn't be quite like the regular workday because you had all sorts of other things going on. By 6 P.M., everybody would be gone and I would sometimes stay very late and sometimes not. One of the things that I began to believe as I looked at those people who were coming in and those who weren't coming was that the people who weren't coming in had good marriages and the people who were coming in didn't.

For me, one of the takeaways from David's story is that how you invest your time matters. If you don't regularly invest time in relationships, they will suffer. When you look at the characteristics that describe how you are at your best, take time to consider how those qualities can inform the routines that will strengthen your most important relationships. One way to do this is to ask yourself, With whom do I have a relationship who could benefit from being with me when I am at my best? This kind of self-examination can lead to some very important decisions about how you choose to invest your time and with whom you choose to invest it. As a coach, I work with clients on a lot of "improvement projects" that come down to mismanaged relationships. Interestingly, their tendency to mismanage relationships is often not limited to the workplace. Time, attention, and tuning in usually form the cure for unhealthy relationships both inside and outside of work.

When you're ready to give more consideration to singling out the routines that, if regularly practiced, would reinforce how you are at your best, write headings for the *Mental, Physical, Spiritual,* and *Relational* domains at the 10:00, 2:00, 4:00, and 8:00 positions around the core characteristics you wrote down earlier. Under each heading, write down three or four routines that apply to that domain and align with your core characteristics.

## Results in Three Arenas of Life

The last step in completing your Life GPS is to consider the goals and intentions you have in the three key life arenas of home, work, and community. A good question to ask yourself in this regard is, If I was clear about how I am at my best and was reinforcing that best state through regularly practicing targeted routines, what would I hope or expect to see manifested in my life at home, at work, and in the broader community? If you're like most of my clients, your answers to this question may yield a few surprises.

As an example, I recently spoke to a chapter of the Young Presidents' Organization and led each of the members through the process of completing a personal Life GPS. When I asked them to share with each other what was surprising or unusual about some of the goals they established in the three life arenas, there were some interesting responses. One participant, the head of a very successful venture capital fund, said that he was struck by the goals he wrote down for the work arena. When he had written work-related goals in the past, his focus had been strictly on metrics and results. On this day, because he had earlier identified one of his at-his-best characteristics as being supportive, he included some work-related goals around creating an environment in which everyone felt relaxed and supported in doing their best work. He immediately noted the connection between a positive work environment and achieving the financial goals that he had solely focused on in the past. This was a first for him and was an insight that he wouldn't have had without stopping to consider the connection between himself at his best and how that could apply to each life arena. He told us that, while he felt he had done a pretty good job of being supportive in the home arena over the years, he had never really thought about applying that characteristic at work. When he turned his attention to the possibility of applying his at-his-best self to all three arenas of life, he immediately saw the potential benefits of taking a more consistently integrated approach in his life.

To complete your Life GPS, write the heading *Home* at the top center of your page and the headings *Work* and *Community* toward the bottom left and right corners respectively. After you've considered the effects of consistently reinforcing how you are at your best, write down three or four outcomes you would expect to see in each of the three arenas of life. When you've finished that step, your Life GPS is complete. Most people find a sense of both power and peace in writing down what is most important to them in life on a single piece of paper.

## Recalibrating Your Course

Commercial aircraft are equipped with automatic pilot systems that make continuous slight adjustments to keep them on course to the planned destination. These minor course corrections counteract factors such as the winds aloft that, if not addressed, can take the plane significantly off course. Now that you have a Life GPS, you can use it as a tool for regularly recalibrating your course through the uncharted terrain of the next level. Take a few minutes each week to bring yourself back to how you are at your best by reviewing and reflecting on your Life GPS. During this time, ask yourself how you're doing with your routines in the four domains. What's working well in reinforcing your core characteristics? What needs more attention or needs to be adjusted? What do you notice happening in the three arenas of your life? Taking this kind of time for review and reflection is a powerful way to pick up the habit of regular renewal of your energy and perspective.

## Keeping Your Perspective

Several years ago, I had the wonderful opportunity to hear Bill Russell deliver keynote remarks at a conference I was attending. With an NCAA championship, an Olympic gold medal, and seven NBA championships with the Boston Celtics to his credit, Russell is one of the most accomplished athletes in any sport. He is also a remarkably thoughtful and warm human being. As a speaker, he projects a relaxed and gracious presence with a generous laugh and stories that evoke both humor and thought. On this occason, he closed his remarks with a story about a trip he was taking with his teammate John Havlicek during the heyday of the Celtics' championship run in the 1960s.

Russell and Havlicek were waiting in an airport lounge for the call to board their flight. As he was sitting there, a woman approached Russell and said, "Hey, you're that famous basketball player, aren't you?" Russell said, "No ma'am, I'm not." A little while later, someone else came up to Russell and again asked if he was a basketball player. Again, Russell said he was not. At that point,

Havlicek leaned over to Russell and asked, "Russ, how come you're telling these people you're not a basketball player?" Russell replied, "Because I'm not. I am Bill Russell. I *play* basketball, but I *am* Bill Russell."

Bill Russell's story has stuck with me as a reminder that all of us are so much more than whatever job we fill. We are each unique individuals with a set of experiences, skills, and characteristics whose potential influence extends far beyond any one job. Remember that on days when you feel tempted to run flat out until you crash. You are not your job. You are who you are and you have the daily opportunity to bring the best of who you are to your life at home and in your community as well as to your job.

**10 TIPS**

**For Picking Up Regular Renewal of Your Energy and Perspective and Letting Go of Running Flat Out Until You Crash**

1. Break the cycle of continuous exertion by building some regular time for recovery into your calendar.

2. Regularly get up on the balcony to see the whole picture of what's going on down on the dance floor.

3. Leave space in your schedule to deal with the unexpected crises that will inevitably demand your best thinking.

4. Make a choice to take the time to establish and practice the routines that bring out the best in you.

5. Develop the confidence to navigate the uncharted terrain of executive life by creating your own Life GPS.

6. Identify the core characteristics that describe how you are at your best.

7. Establish routines in the mental, physical, spiritual, and relational domains that reinforce how you are at your best.

8. Write down what you would expect or hope to see in the arenas of home, work, and community if you were consistently performing at your best.

9. Recalibrate your course through uncharted terrain by regularly reviewing your Life GPS and assessing your performance against it.

10. Keep your perspective by remembering that you are not your job.

# 4

## PICK UP CUSTOM-FIT COMMUNICATIONS

## LET GO OF ONE-SIZE-FITS-ALL COMMUNICATIONS

I remember early in my career as an executive trying to explain to my son Andy, who was six or seven at the time, what I did in my job all day. Thinking about all the meetings I either convened or attended, the presentations and speeches I gave, the phone calls I made and the conversations with colleagues, I told Andy that I basically got paid for talking to people. That explanation oversimplified things a little bit but not by much. In my coaching work with executives, most of what we focus on eventually comes back to some aspect of communication. When you think about it, executives don't spend much of their time producing anything tangible. They produce and deal in ideas. For those ideas to be of any value, they have to be well communicated to the right audiences at the right time.

## Aligning Your Audience with Your Outcome

When I coach, I regularly ask clients, "What result are you trying to achieve?" This is a question that relates not just to big-picture goals but to the process of communicating with colleagues. I believe that effective communication is strategic and intentional. When I am working with my clients on communication effectiveness, I want them to think about the audience for their message. I ask them to be clear about what they want the members of the audience to think after hearing their message: What is the key idea that they should take away from the communication? I then ask my clients to consider how they want their audience to feel as a result of the communication: Should they feel excited, challenged, motivated, energized, or some other emotion? Then I ask clients to consider: What action do you want the audience to take based on that emotional state? And, getting back to the original question: What result are you trying to achieve through their action?

I have seen this sort of strategic approach to communication work again and again in organizations. A couple of months ago, I saw a great illustration of how it works in other aspects of life. When Johnny Carson, longtime host of the *Tonight Show,* died, Jay Leno and David Letterman both dedicated an evening of their shows to remembering the King of Late Night. The last guest on Leno's tribute was comedian Drew Carey. As part of his time with Carey, Leno showed a clip from Carey's first appearance as a stand-up comic on Carson's show. For thirty years, the goal of all comedians was to get a guest shot on the *Tonight Show* and to be so funny that Carson called them over to the couch for a brief chat after their routine. As the video showed Carey finishing up his bit, he hesitantly glanced over to Carson and got the nod to come over. Carey's response to the wave over was to do an almost double-take while he brought his hand to his chest in a "Who, me?" kind of gesture. When the clip was over, Leno noted Carey's reaction and asked him if he was surprised to be called over. "Yeah, I was," Carey said, "but here's the thing. When I found out I was going to be booked on the show, I spent six weeks by myself going over my routine word for word just visualizing how it would go, the audience's reaction, Johnny's reaction. It would always end with Johnny saying, 'That's very funny stuff' and then calling me over to the couch. I just went through that process over and over for six weeks. When it happened exactly the way I practiced it, I couldn't believe it."

Drew Carey essentially went through the same swing thought again and again in the six weeks before he appeared on the *Tonight Show*. By sharing this story, I'm certainly not suggesting that you practice six weeks for every presentation. You would never get anything else done! What I am encouraging, however, is that you be very clear about your desired outcome, the audience for your message, and what it will take to move that audience toward your desired outcome. This is what custom-fit communications means. Effective executives think strategically about their communications and custom-fit their approach to take into account where their audience is and where they want their audience to be in terms of thought, feeling, and action. Recognizing that audiences are different, they know that practicing a one-size-fits-all approach to communication will rarely lead to the results they hope to achieve. Within your organization, you will regularly communicate as an executive with a number of different audiences:

- The organization as a whole

- Your boss

- Other senior executives

- Your executive-level peers

- Your functional team

While effective communication will be an ongoing theme in other chapters of this book (especially the chapters on defining what to do, looking left and right as you lead, and picking up a big-footprint view of your role), it makes sense to look at some principles and advice from our executive mentors that can be applied to custom-fitting your communications for these key audiences.

## Communicating with the Whole Organization

As an executive, you are always on stage in your organization. As a result, you need to be much more aware of the impact of your communications than you may have been in the past. When I asked her to think about the things that changed most when she became an executive, Donna Morea of CGI-AMS noted that she realized she could be much more casual about her communications before she became an executive than she could after she was promoted to the next level. Because the entire organization pays attention to what executives say and do, Morea says, "You have to be consistently engaged. You can't casually complain aloud about some bureaucratic aspect of the company or problems with a client or make an offhand remark about someone. All of that is taboo."

### Watch Your Impact

Martin Carter, president of Hydro Aluminum North America, shared Morea's point of view and expanded on it in our interview. He provides an excellent case study of an executive who was aware that his natural style of communication was not always appropriate to the needs of the audience or where he needed the audience to go. During his years as an executive, Carter has combined self-awareness with intention around positive changes he wanted to make in his communication style. In our interview, I asked him first to describe what prompted the changes in his communication style when he reached the executive level:

I noticed that you have to be very deliberate in communication. In previous roles I have had, I could be a little bit off-the-wall in terms of the way I communicate things [with my peers] because these are colleagues with whom I collaborate. You have to be very careful in how you communicate outside of that group. It's not that you can't be informal and relaxed, but [you have to remember that] what you say tends to be quoted and stated and used very actively in the organization. So I watch that much more than I did previously.

When I asked Carter for an example of what caused him to notice the different dynamics around communication at the executive level, he told me about visiting a Hydro plant and making a casual comment about the size of the plant's maintenance budget. A month or so later, he noticed that the maintenance budget for that plant had been dramatically reduced—when all he meant to convey during his visit was that the staff should take a look at it. On more than one occasion, Carter told me, he learned that if he pushed a point too hard, people would act on it even if it really wasn't in the best interest of that particular business unit. He found that as an executive his comments were often taken too literally.

## Encourage Rich Dialogue

Carter has found that the antidote to this communication challenge is to cultivate a more informal presence when he is out in the organization. As an Englishman working for a Scandinavian company, Carter has found that this approach is needed more in the United States than in Europe. Carter notes, "[It is] absolutely acceptable in northern European culture to push back heavily on leaders and to see no consequence for that. That is accepted as a norm. In the United States, that is just not the case and in Britain that isn't so much the case either. So something that I have had to watch is that I need to think about how I communicate and encourage much more informality with people."

## Cultivate Informality

While Martin Carter has learned to custom-fit his communications to be more effective within the U.S. workplace culture, his approach also applies to learning how to adjust from one company culture to another. Depending on the history of the industry and the particular company, a communication culture can be relatively more open or closed. Open communication cultures are almost always more effective in terms of productively engaging employees in surfacing both opportunities and problems in a way that they can be acted on. As an executive, you have the opportunity to help shape the communication culture of your company through the way you handle your communications in the broader organization. If you want to sustain or build an open culture, seek to put people at all levels at ease. Even if this does not come naturally to you, it is possible to develop this approach by being clear about what you're trying to do and intentionally adopting some behaviors that reinforce your goal. Here's how Carter describes his development process in learning to be a more relaxed executive communicator with employees throughout the organization:

> Really, what I was after was much more informality so that we could get much better dialogue. That's something that I have had to work on myself to make sure that people don't, when they feel challenged by me, just take that as a call to action rather than a call to think. I try to put people at ease. It is extremely important for them to feel that they are in an environment in which we can discuss difficult issues and they can put their views on the table. I try to encourage this by using as examples mistakes that I have made or wrong decisions that I have made. I am there . . . to challenge and encourage and to get people to think about what they are doing and to think a little bit differently about the things they may be dealing with from one day to the other—and not just to take it as an absolute direction from me.

## Create Connection

What Carter describes is an approach to communication that establishes him as a human being first and an executive second. By acknowledging mistakes and poor decisions he has made, he demonstrates to the organization that he has his ego under control and is willing to make himself vulnerable to encourage others to relax and open up. In *Primal Leadership,* emotional intelligence expert Daniel Goleman and coauthors describe the approach that Martin Carter takes to employee communication as an *affiliative* style of leadership. By opening himself up, Carter establishes affiliation, or connection, with the people he leads. In my observations, the affiliative style of leadership communication is often underused when compared to other styles—such as *visionary, commanding,* or *pacesetting*—identified by Goleman and his colleagues. In this final quote, Martin Carter describes in more detail what he does to establish affiliative communications when he is with employees throughout his company:

[My goal is to take] as much formality out of meetings as possible. Once you have an executive title, you are treated absolutely differently and more often than not without any good reason—except that you have authority to affect people's lives.

We are in a position to affect people's lives. That means that people clam up and they tend to be much more formal. They tend to be much more rigid. They are trying to paint a rosy picture on things that are, frankly, not a rosy picture. They tend to focus on the positive rather than the hard issues. So you really have to create a work environment in which that is not the case. There are very simple things you can do to encourage this, like having dinner with the team the night before you have the meeting. Or having lunch with them so you can relax and talk about family and football and whatever you do. I'm not going to attend plant meetings as Europeans tend to with a suit and

tie on. I want to create a relaxed setting. I want to show a genuine interest in not only the business but the individuals themselves. So we, as an executive team, not just me, spend a lot
of time showing genuine interest in that individual, or in, you
know, where their son or their daughter is going to college.

Through his dress, the content and style of his questions, and the
ways in which he spends time with employees, Carter promotes an
environment in which people feel safe to contribute and offer their
honest assessments in conversation. One result of that is that he and
his fellow executives get the information they need to run the business much more effectively.

## Communicating with Your Boss

Because of the increase in the number of audiences or constituencies
with whom you need to communicate, one of the most precious
resources you will have as an executive is your time. If you find that
managing your time is challenging for you as a new executive, imagine what it is like for your boss. As a more senior executive, your
boss is likely attending to even more constituencies than you are and
will almost certainly be dealing with members of your company's
board of directors, as well as key external stakeholders such as customers, business partners, and regulatory agencies. You may be dealing with representatives from some or all of these groups, but the
likelihood is that the stakes are higher in your boss's conversations
than they are in yours. And, while managing these types of relationships, your boss is also responsible for communicating to many of the
same audiences that you are dealing with. The point here is that you
need to be intentional and focused in communicating with your boss.
At the executive level, you will probably find that you have less face-
to-face time with your boss than you did with your managers earlier
in your career. It is therefore important to make the most of the time
you do have and to find effective alternative ways to supplement that

time to keep the lines of communication open between the two of you.

## Agree on a Process and a Framework

Don't wait for your boss to tell you what information you're supposed to provide and how often you're supposed to provide it. Ask. If, earlier in your career, you developed a process for keeping your boss informed that worked for the two of you, ask your new boss if that same process would work now. Determine the communication style your boss prefers and be consistent. Is it e-mail, voice mail, conference calls, or regular face-to-face meetings? Do what you can to understand the level of detail your boss is looking for. Is it just the headlines with a short summary or is it more detail on the issues?

To make it easy to process and act on your information, out of the flood of data that is coming into your boss's office, adopt a simple and consistent framework for presenting it. University of Michigan business professor David Ulrich offers a communication framework that is built on three simple questions:

- *What?* What issue needs to be addressed or considered?

- *So What?* What are the implications of this issue that make it worthy of consideration?

- *Now What?* What needs to be done next about this issue? What action or support do you need from your boss? What milestones should your boss look for in terms of progress?

Of course, communication between you and your boss will flow in two directions. I have found that the What?—So What?—Now What? framework is a simple and effective checklist to use when you're receiving information as well. Asking the kinds of open-ended questions associated with the framework leads to better understanding and clarity around the issues and the expectations for follow-up action.

## Leverage Your Boss's Communication Profile

The ideal scenario is when you and your boss are communicating with each other so effectively that you understand the kind of information your boss needs to further his or her agenda in the organization. By providing regular updates on progress against goals or early warnings on issues that need to be addressed, you can make your boss's work much easier. At the same time, your boss is in a position to leverage his or her communication with senior peers and the next level up (be it the CEO, the board, or other representatives of the most senior level of leadership) on behalf of the agenda you and your functional team are pursuing. One of the newer executives I interviewed described how this symbiotic communication relationship works between him and his boss:

> I went from reporting to a vice president to a senior vice president. When I made that transition, I made it a point to talk to my SVP and ask, 'Would this communications process work for you?' While she didn't ask for it, I found that by offering a way to communicate how things are going that it worked very well for her. So we are continuing that process and I'm finding that she is running with it. I regularly see her forwarding my e-mails on to her boss, the president. He'll respond back to her and then she'll respond back to my team with congratulatory remarks. . . . While my team wants to know that I am happy with their performance, there is also a need for them to feel like their performance is being recognized at levels above. It is motivational for my team to see that my boss sees what they are doing and that they know that I am letting our boss see that. Especially in big organizations, while your boss has a lot to say about your performance ratings, it is usually your team's rating versus other teams' ratings. Your team needs to know that their performance is being seen at the higher levels.

This quote includes a number of important points. First, by providing regular updates on substantive progress, the executive who shared this with me is positioning his boss to look good in front of her bosses. Second, his boss is then able to use the positive feedback she receives from above to motivate her direct report's team. Third, through regularly providing updates to his boss, my executive friend is managing the communication flow to enable his boss to speak from a position of strength when it comes time to advocate for his team's performance in comparison with that of other teams in the organization. All told, this is a great example of how a strong communication process can leverage the profile and strengthen the agenda of both sides of a reporting relationship.

## Speak for the Work

I often meet managers who believe that if they do good work, it will speak for itself and good things will happen. This may be true in the lower levels of the organization, but it is not true at the executive levels. The truth is that most senior executives are simply too busy to notice unless success is pointed out to them. It is important to remember that at the next level, the work doesn't speak for itself; you have to speak for the work. As the extended quote that I just shared indicates, it is important to craft and implement an ongoing strategy of keeping the results of your team's good work in front of your boss and your boss's senior executive peers.

Please note the distinction here that the work you are speaking for is your team's work and not your own. Nothing turns off senior executives more quickly than a braggart who claims all the credit for a team's accomplishments. At the executive level, one of your jobs is to position your functional team for success. When they are successful, your next job is to speak for their success. This is the point at which your personal work *will* speak for itself. If your team is seen as successful, their success will be attributed to you without your having to claim it for yourself. In addition to the benefits of recognition for your team, regularly speaking for the work also has the positive effect of making your executive leaders more comfortable with what's going on. With that in mind, here is some advice on how to speak for your team's work from the same executive who talked about how he partners with his boss on communications:

> It is important to share your successes upwards. When I was a group manager, our results were seen a lot more frequently by our director because we had a lot more exposure to him. At the executive level, they don't always see your successes. They certainly know when you have a miss or something is not hitting a number like it is supposed to. But they don't always see the successes. I've found that it really helps to make sure I share the challenges that we've overcome to make something happen and just what that success was. That really gives my senior leadership much more perspective about what the team is accomplishing.
>
> [To avoid the appearance of bragging,] I work it out with my boss and her boss. They want to know what is going on, so I work that in when I do a regular update and give them a good sound bite. I might send them an e-mail bulletin and say here are some things that we have accomplished and here are some of the challenges that we faced. They, in turn, pass those sound bites on to the next level. I have also found that when I can share that kind of information with my bosses they feel more comfortable staying less involved. In the very beginning, I felt like there was more pressure from them because they wanted to be more involved and wanted to know what was going on. As we got that process working where I sent regular updates they started backing off because they could see the results and they had information that they could pass on. That took pressure off of me and my team.

## Communicating with Senior Executives

As a new executive, you may feel like you are constantly being assessed and evaluated. If you feel this way, then you probably are.

One of the primary responsibilities of the most senior executives in an organization is to identify and develop their potential successors. If you have aspirations of continuing to move up in your organization (and even if you don't), approach your communications with more senior executives as an opportunity to create and leave an impression of confident competence. In conducting feedback for clients, I regularly hear a few key points that can help you create this impression without trying to turn your natural personality into something it is not.

## Listen

In the rush to make a contribution, it is easy to forget to listen. Slow down and get the lay of the land before rushing in to offer your opinion or point of view. Cultivate the habit of asking open-ended questions to learn what is most important to your organization's most senior executives. Take time to ask what success looks like to them. Align your actions with their definition of success. In the world of sales, this practice is called *needs-based selling;* it works just as well when what you're selling is how you add value to the organization.

## Prepare to Make Positive Impressions

Your opportunities to make positive impressions on senior executives will come in formal presentations, regular update meetings, and more informal conversations. Whatever the venue, it is important to be prepared with a point of view on the key issues facing not just your function but the company as a whole. As Mike Lanier of Verizon told me, "When you get this exposure, make sure you have the right preparation. You don't want to go in there and have one of your off days." Sue Stephenson, a senior vice president at the Ritz Carlton Company, echoed Lanier's thoughts, saying, "It is almost disrespectful to not do the pre-work before you meet with the group."

Chapters 8 and 9 present a lot of valuable perspective and advice on how to prepare to present your point of view. In the context of thinking about custom-fitting your communication to a senior executive audience, it is important that you be prepared to discuss your key issues at any time. One good method for doing this kind of preparation is to regularly review your short list of key initiatives and priorities and have a brief speech ready to deliver when a senior executive asks you what you're working on. You're probably familiar with the idea of an *elevator speech,* a brief pitch you could deliver in the length of an elevator ride. In developing General Electric's change acceleration process in the early 1990's, a team of external consultants came up with the following four-step format for developing effective elevator speeches:

**1.** Our project or initiative is about . . .

**2.** It is critical to the company because . . .

**3.** What this means for you is . . .

**4.** Here's how you can help . . .

You can see how this format aligns with the What?—So What?—Now What? framework I introduced earlier in this chapter. Point 1 addresses what is happening, points 2 and 3 outline the implications on the organizational and personal levels, and point 4 moves the action forward by making a request for help. If you haven't done so already, I encourage you to set aside some time in the next couple of days to identify your top three or four issues and develop an elevator speech for each of them.

## Keep It Crisp

One of the reasons a format like the elevator speech is so helpful in communicating with senior executives is that it compels you to organize your thinking into succinct statements. In your everyday communication with senior executives, it is important to keep it crisp and to the point. As is likely the case with your boss, the typical senior executive is very busy. Usually they will expect you to cut to the chase in your conversations. Prepare for this by organizing your thinking and boiling it down to the main points before meeting with the senior executives of your organization.

## Speak in Terms of Solutions, Not Problems

While good senior executives will not expect you to be a yes-man or yes-woman in conversation, they will usually expect you to present a positive, can-do approach to dealing with problems. Donna Morea, president of CGI-AMS, explains what she looks for from her executives in this regard:

> I think the way that you express doubt is very important. It requires thoughtfulness and finesse. As an executive, you are somebody who the world is looking to to lead. If you are worried about something, have doubts about something, or are questioning something, that just gets magnified. The art is to acknowledge challenges and weaknesses but always in the context of constructive solution building. You can't gripe just to blow off steam like you may have done as a lower-level manager. You can acknowledge a problem but you have to either have a plan or move quickly to have a plan to address it.

Some new executives I've known have had a tendency to "catastrophize" aloud about everything that could go wrong in a given situation. This was the way they processed issues for themselves; but they failed to realize that, by doing this in front of more senior executives, they were leaving the impression that things were far worse than they really were. Moreover, they were leaving impressions of themselves as people mired in the depths of depression rather than as leaders who could work their way through a problem. Check yourself on this issue and, if you find that you have this habit, work on keeping your doomsday thinking to yourself.

## Establish the Context

When explaining your results and progress to senior executives, you will have more success in garnering their support and recognition if you take some time to establish and explain the context of your work. One Fortune 500 executive I interviewed for this book succeeded a predecessor who was fired because he didn't establish the context for his work for the senior executives in his organization. The current executive has been very successful in the same position and attributes much of his success to helping his senior executives understand the progress that he and his team have made. In our interview, he contrasted his approach with that of his predecessor:

> The guy in the job before me just let the numbers show up on a piece of paper and most of the senior management was not as close to what all of those numbers meant. They knew what the numbers meant versus what the objective was but they didn't know what they meant versus what the environment around them was or what it took to deliver those numbers in an environment where your budget was cut by 50 percent. The results senior management saw didn't count as much as they should have because my predecessor didn't take the time to really position things and help everybody understand the context of those results. The senior execs just saw the numbers on paper and based their judgment on that.

> What I've spent time doing is explaining how we are doing versus the market. I talk about how we are doing versus where we were before. I work to put the results in perspective. I am just doing constant framing of what the results really mean. The team I have is the same team that was in place before and they were delivering on a high level prior to my taking the leadership role, but I just don't think my predecessor did as good of a job as he should have in making sure the organization understood the context of his team's performance.

# Presenting to Senior Executives

Given that delivering formal presentations is a regular part of executive life, it's sort of amazing how few executives are really good at it. Honestly, how many outstanding business presentations have you sat through in your career? If you're like most people, the answer is not many. By custom-fitting your presentations for your audience, you have an opportunity to differentiate yourself from other executive leaders and accomplish a lot more for your organization. While there are lots of resources available to learn how to be a better speaker, the executive mentors I spoke with offered some principles that, if practiced, will make you a more effective communicator in presenting to senior executives.

## Be Clear About What You're Trying to Accomplish

To help clients preparing for an important presentation or meeting get to the essence of custom-fit communications, I always ask them what they're trying to accomplish in the meeting. To clarify their desired outcome, I follow up by asking, "At the end of the meeting, what do you want the audience to think? How do you want them to feel? What do you want them to do?" Asking and answering these questions yourself will provide some clarity around what you're trying to accomplish.

## Prepare for the Audience

Mike Lanier of Verizon says that, in preparing for his presentations to senior executives, he tries to put himself in the shoes of each of them and understand the business case from their point of view. He tries to identify what the likely pain points are going to be for them and the elements of his proposals that represent success for them. What are the things that your executives want to hear or need to hear? What would they be likely to support? What would it take to win their support?

Bill Christopher is vice president of McKesson Process Technologies (MPT), a business unit of McKesson Corporation. His job requires him to both regularly deliver presentations to senior executives and sit through the presentations of his peers. Based on his experience, he has come up with the following principles for preparing successful presentations to senior executives:

- In preparing to present to senior executives, first learn how they think and the style and approach they prefer.

  *Are they visual or verbal? Bottom-line or big-picture strategic? Are they into Excel spreadsheets or PowerPoint presentations? Shape your approach to appeal to their preferred style of receiving information.*

- Talk with peers who have already presented to them.

  *What was approved? What was the style and content of the presentations and proposals that were approved?*

- Remember that form will likely come before function.

  *Junior executives that deliver presentations that look better and are presented more professionally get more positive attention than those that come in with sloppy presentations, even though they might have a better idea.*

## Focus on What, Not How

Ed Sannini of Morgan Stanley notes that senior executives will, unless given a reason to think otherwise, assume that the processes that led to a conclusion or recommendation are sound and correct. So, you do not need to spend a lot of time in your presentation explaining the nuts and bolts of how you came to your conclusion. As

Sannini said to me, "When you go to a senior executive presentation, their expectation is tell me what it means, don't tell me how you put the answer together." A common mistake that new executives make is to focus too much on how they came to their conclusions. To do this is to risk getting labeled as someone who, when asked for the time, explains how to build a watch. Focus much more on your recommendations and their implications than on the mechanics of how you arrived at them.

## Remember That Less Is Usually More

If you focus on what more than how, you will likely avoid the mistake of including too much detail in your presentation. In the age of PowerPoint, too many presenters overload their audiences with graph after graph and bullet after bullet. Enough already! Really think about what needs to be said to reach your audience and get them to your desired outcome. Certainly, anticipate the questions you might be asked and be prepared with solid answers—but don't try to anticipate every single question with its answering PowerPoint slide. To do so is to risk losing your audience in the weeds of detail and not leave space for dealing with the primary objectives of your presentation. Leave space for a conversation and an exchange of ideas. You will learn more and so will your audience.

## Tell a Story

Earlier, one of our executive mentors made a great point about the importance of establishing context around your results. The same point holds in making presentations. Your points and recommendations will be better received if you establish the context for them. A great way to do that is to tell a story. Think for a moment about the best speakers you've heard inside and outside the business world. What was it about these speakers that made you sit up and really listen? What did they say that caused you to remember what they said?

Was it the numbers and the analysis that spoke to your head or was it a story that spoke to your emotions? When you are preparing a presentation, take some extra time to identify the story behind the presentation. In a 2003 interview in *Harvard Business Review,* screenwriter Robert McKee made the point that all good stories deal with a challenge that has to be overcome and the struggles that the protagonist has to deal with to achieve ultimate victory. The original *Star Wars* trilogy provides an example of this approach to storytelling. In the real world, Martin Luther King Jr.'s "I Have a Dream" speech demonstrates the power of storytelling. While your issues probably won't be as dramatic as Luke Skywalker's or as profound as King's, use storytelling to appeal to your audience. Open your presentation with a brief story that illustrates what success will look like, the barriers that will have to be overcome to achieve it, and the actions required to achieve the goal in spite of those barriers. If this feels uncomfortable, start small and observe the reactions of your audience. In all likelihood, they will appreciate the momentary respite from one more PowerPoint slide and the chance to engage the imaginative, as well as the logical, part of their brain.

## Communicating with Peers

Later in this book, I talk about picking up the habit of looking left and right as you lead and letting go of the habit of looking primarily up and down as you lead. By looking left and right, I mean paying attention to the agendas, needs, and wants of your executive peers. At the executive level, communication with peers is critical because so much of what you need to accomplish depends on their cooperation and collaboration with you. Jason Jeffay of Hewitt Associates makes the point clearly: "Too often, we think of communication as information. Communication is much more around influence and direction." Stephen Cerrone, a senior vice president with JP Morgan

Chase, builds on Jeffay's observation by noting, "The ability to influence versus control . . . requires appreciation of other people's styles." As is the case with the other audiences discussed in this chapter, effective communication with your peers requires a custom-fit approach tailored to their styles and interests.

## Communicating with Your Team

Your functional team should be your first line of defense in alerting you to issues that need your attention and your first line of offense in creating the action required to achieve results. The foundation of your success as an executive is the strength of your functional team. There is so much to say about this that Chapters 5, 6, and 7 are dedicated to the topic.

### Take the Time

In the context of custom-fitting your communications to your functional team, I want to highlight a common mistake that new executives make. With the increase in expectations and demands on your time that emerge at the executive level, it is all too easy to ignore or overlook communications with your team. This is a mistake that I made as a new executive and that I regularly see committed by other executives. The custom-fit communication advice I would offer with regard to your functional team is to be intentional about creating time to be approachable and available to them. Schedule time for regular and frequent conversations with your direct reports. Take time to walk the floor or go to remote locations to be visible to the folks on the front line. Before you have the meetings and make the visits, take the time to think about the message you want to deliver and the impression you want to leave. During the meeting or the visit, be present. Ignore the phone and the e-mail. Quit looking at your watch every few minutes. Send signals that suggest you are fully engaged and ready to listen to what people have to say. Taking these steps with your functional team will create the kind of free-flowing communication environment that will make the rest of your life as an executive much easier.

## Presence Begets Presence

As this chapter concludes, I want to come back to the idea that presence begets presence. As an executive, you are in a very visible position in your organization. Whether you recognize it or not, people are watching you—and whether they recognize it or not, they will follow your lead. Your presence as a leader will play a large part in determining the presence of those being led. Daniel Goleman likes to say that emotions are contagious. If you show up as positive and optimistic, those around you will likely reflect that presence. Conversely, it doesn't take long for negativity emanating from a leader to spread throughout an organization.

A number of years ago, UCLA professor Albert Mehrabian conducted a study to determine the factors that were most important in how audiences process information from a speaker. Mehrabian found three key factors: the content of the presentation, the speaker's body language, and the speaker's tone of voice. Of these, body language was responsible for 55 percent of the impact of the presentation; tone of voice for 38 percent, and content for only 7 percent. The point is clear; people pay much more attention to the subtle emotional cues in communication than they do to what is actually said. The implications for you as an executive leader and communicator are also clear. To communicate what you intend to communicate, you have to manage your presence at least as much as the content of your message. If you want people to be excited about the future, then your tone of voice and body language have to project excitement. You can't just say you're excited; they need to see it and hear it. To be fully effective with each of the multiple audiences you're reaching as an executive, you must be conscious of your presence and intentional in managing it. When it comes to communicationm and leadership, it helps to remember this aphorism: Your actions speak so loudly that I can't hear what you're saying.

(10 **TIPS**)   **For Picking Up Custom-Fit Communications and Letting Go of One-Size-Fits-All Communications**

1   Custom-fit your communication approach to the audience and to the result you're trying to achieve.

2   Take into account where your audience is and where you want them to be in terms of thought, feeling, and action.

3   Be intentional about your communications; create an environment in which people feel safe to share information.

4   Establish a process of regular communication with your boss that is easy and effective for both of you.

5   Create opportunities to speak for the good work of your team and position your boss to share that information with peers and superiors.

6   Listen to the concerns and priorities of senior executives before rushing in with your opinion or plan of action.

7   Package your key issues and initiatives in crisp sound bites that outline their importance and the actions required for success.

8   Share your results in a context that enables others to understand progress made and challenges overcome.

9   Do your homework before important presentations by learning what is most important to the audience and the methods of communication that work best for them.

10   Remember that presence begets presence. People will take more cues from your body language and tone of voice than they will from your content.

# The Foundations of
# Team Presence

# PICK UP TEAM RELIANCE

# LET GO OF SELF-RELIANCE

Beginning with this chapter, we build on the foundations of personal presence and move on to creating success through team presence. By team presence, I mean the work you do with your functional team as opposed to the work you do as an executive in the broader organization. In this chapter and the next two, we'll talk about three sets of behaviors to pick up and three sets of behaviors to let go of for executives leading functional teams. We'll get to the issues of defining what to do (in Chapter 6) and picking up accountability (in Chapter 7) for many results, but let's start with picking up the habit of team reliance and letting go of the habit of self-reliance. Making this shift sounds simple, but it can be one of the toughest for new executives to make. If you fit the profile of most new executives, the superstar individual or team leader who has been promoted to the next level, you are going to have to make that comfort shift we talked about in Chapter 2: letting go of reliance on your functional expertise. For a number of reasons, many new executives stumble and fall on the rocks of not learning to rely on their team to accomplish the results that matter most.

Marc Effron, a partner with Hewitt Associates, is the leader of his firm's annual study of the top twenty companies for developing leaders. In talking with me about what it takes to be successful at the next level, he offered this perspective:

> I think it is one thing to be a headstrong individual contributor and know what you are good at, and you can go a long way doing that. There are a lot of very strong individual contributors at the middle manager level who aren't self-aware, but they certainly know what they can do on a daily basis and they are very good at it. I think when you get to any senior level in an organization you have broader responsibilities. [To succeed at the executive level,] you simply have to understand more comprehensively your own strengths and weaknesses . . . because it is a fairly well-validated fact and somewhat commonsense as well that we don't succeed at the executive level because of additional functional strengths. We succeed because we start to eliminate some of the derailers that have always been with us in our career.

Effron makes a number of important points here. To move successfully to the executive level, you have to develop a heightened level of awareness around your strengths and weaknesses. The most effective executives are those who understand the strengths that top-level leadership requires as well as those that, when overused, can become weaknesses. As Effron says, because of the broader responsibilities you have as an executive, you now have to turn over the day-to-day execution of functional responsibilities to your team. One of the biggest derailers is trying to do all the functional work yourself once you become an executive. Self-reliance may have worked for you in the past, but you have to let it go now or you will be under water so quickly that it may be tough to recover.

Mike Lanier of Verizon summed up the nature of the shift quite succinctly when he said that you have to shift from being the go-to person who makes sure everything is buttoned up to having a team of go-to people working for you who make sure a much broader range of things are buttoned up. The results expected from executives are simply too broad for any one person to do.

## Get Your Ego Out of the Way

One of the biggest barriers to shifting away from functional responsibilities is likely to be your ego. As human beings, almost all of us enjoy praise and recognition. If you've made it to the executive level, or are close to moving there, you have almost certainly received a lot of positive feedback for your ability to get things done and make things happen. Have you noticed that your ego likes that and wants more of it? In a way, your ego acts as the counterweight to your inner critic. Instead of discouraging you from acting by reminding you of past failures as the inner critic does, the ego encourages you to act by saying things like "No one else can do this as well as you can," or "If you want a job done right, you have to do it yourself." Ironically, your ego might just be right: Maybe no one does it better than you do. *That does not matter.* To succeed as an executive you have to turn the work over to your team anyway, even if, today, they cannot do it as well as you.

Lucien Alziari has seen dozens of high-potential leaders rise to the executive level during his career at PepsiCo and now at Avon. I want to share with you a few extended thoughts from Alziari because he offers a wonderful reality check to assess where you are in terms of your readiness and willingness to rely on your team:

At the [manager] level the shift is already beginning to take place where the company should rightly assume that the functional skills are in place. That is what got you there and what they are looking for then is more of an emphasis on broader organizational and leadership skills. The shift in those two is much more significant when you go to the [executive] level. . . . The classic lesson is that *the skills that got you to the role are not the skills that are going to make you successful in the role.* And so you can't distinguish yourself or actually even be successful as a vice president just by being good in terms of the functional expertise that the role requires, because that is really what I would call a baseline assumption. People assume that you've got it. If you don't have it, that is a real problem, but if you've got lots of it, that isn't going to distinguish you from everybody else because they've got it too.

In terms of leading your own function, at a vice president level you are managing a team, hopefully, of functional experts themselves, so the role shifts. . . . The skill there has to become how do you work with that team to define the agenda for that group so that the mission, the longer-term strategies, and the priorities are clear. . . . Then, once people are clear about their part in the game, your role is much more of a coach and a counselor. It absolutely isn't doing their jobs for them. The good leaders figure that out. The ones that fail don't, and they end up micromanaging or getting overexposed in terms of the number of commitments they make because they are trying to do everybody else's job for them.

## Assess Your Readiness

What is your assessment of where you are on the path described by Lucien Alziari? Have you figured out yet how to define and turn over the work to the team or are you still relying mainly on your functional expertise? Another aspect of how ego comes into play in making this a difficult shift is that you have probably enjoyed what you've been doing up until now. You have built your functional skills over the years and are probably known in your company and in the marketplace as an expert at what you do. Your sense of identity can get wrapped up in being the expert that everyone relies on or goes to to get the result.

This is a big issue for many of my clients who are just below the executive level in their companies and have been identified as strong candidates to move up. When I conduct colleague feedback for them, I usually hear a desire for the client to contribute on a broader playing field because their colleagues believe they are capable of making contributions that extend far beyond their expertise. It can feel like a leap of faith for these clients to turn over the field in which they've been successful to their teams so they can free up the space for themselves to contribute at the next level. This is the essence of the challenge of moving to the next level. It is about learning to allow your comfort and confidence to flow from the characteristics of how you are at your best rather than continuing to flow from the functional expertise that brought you this far.

## Don't Compete with Your Team

Paul McDermott, now a vice president, was recruited to mortgage giant Freddie Mac several years ago, following a successful career as a high-volume producer in the commercial real estate market in Washington, D.C. When I interviewed him, he talked about the shift you have to make when you move from the role of expert to executive leader: "What made me successful as an individual producer was that I was very focused . . . but when you get to the senior executive level it is about lifting the team." Often, people who are highly successful as individual contributors rely on an internal competitive drive that pushes them to achieve more than their peers. It's safe to say that a lot of people who wind up in the executive ranks have this drive. But, those who have long-term success at the highest levels get their competitive ego under control. They direct their competitive drive to the external world and collaborate internally. This shift has to start with their own teams. As Sid Fuchs of Northrop Grumman says, "Often when team players work and play on the same team, they are in some sort of competition with each other. I think as you [reach] the executive level you need to realize that you can't compete with your team. The way you get your satisfaction and your merit is based on how well you do in helping the team succeed."

Hundreds of books have been written on how to build and lead teams—this is not one of them. There are, however, some important factors for new executives to consider as they position their functional teams to succeed for the good of the company, the team, and themselves. We'll cover some of these in this chapter and deal with additional aspects of executive functional team leadership in Chapters 6 and 7. Here, we'll cover these key concepts:

- Get the right people in the right roles.

- Change out those who don't fit.

- Redefine how you add value.

- Build and lead so that the team is really a team.

## Get the Right People in the Right Roles

There is a reason that the phrase "surround yourself with good people" has become a cliché. In any organization, whether it's business, political, military, or nonprofit, the leader is only going to be as successful as the people being led. This is especially true for leaders at the executive level. The pace is quicker and the demands are greater when you are an executive. You need people on your team who can keep up and contribute to creating successful outcomes. A few months ago, I was bringing my eleven-year-old son, Brad, home from a soccer practice with a team that we thought he might try out for at the beginning of the season. Because Brad has an August birthday, he has "played up" a year in both school and soccer since first grade. That has worked out well for him in school but it has started to catch up with him lately in soccer. The twelve-year-olds he is playing with have all grown half a foot in the past year while Brad has held steady as an already small eleven-year-old. Sensing that he was a little bit intimidated by the new conditions, I asked him on the way home that night what he thought about trying out for this team. He said he wasn't sure and when I asked him why, he said, "It's gotten a lot faster, Dad."

We were able to help Brad by finding a slower league for him to play in until his body catches up with his skills. What he said about soccer being faster is what you'll find at the executive level. But, you can't opt for a slower league, so you have to have a team that can keep up with the pace. By working with and recruiting great people to your team, you will find and feel like you are playing offense much more often than defense. Lucien Alziari says, "[It's like] English football or soccer where if you just watch the game being played it is very, very fluid and people are playing multiple positions in a very intuitive way because they realize that is what they need to do to help their fellow team members and that is what will make the team successful as a whole." If you have not had a truly great team before, it's hard to imagine the positive impact one can have on the results and the quality of life you experience as an executive.

When Mark Stavish joined AOL as its HR leader, he was taking his first senior executive role following a successful career at a number of Fortune 500 companies. In talking with me about the importance of assembling a strong team at AOL, he said, "I quickly realized I had to hire people who knew a whole lot more about things than I did. And then my role was to try to figure out how to orchestrate it and be the external salesperson to the rest of the organization."

## Change Out Those Who Don't Fit

In my own case, when I joined Columbia Gas Transmission as VP of human resources, I inherited a functional team that had largely been in place for many years—working for a series of executives who managed them as a traditional HR department. As part of a management team that was brought in to bring the company out of bankruptcy, my boss, company president and CEO Cathy Abbott, was clear that she wanted to transform the company culture away from the mind-set of a regulated utility into that of an innovative company generating higher-than-average returns on invested capital. Her expectation was that HR would play a major role in that culture change and she recruited me to help lead that effort. I was fortunate in that I had some very-high-potential people on my team who were just waiting to show what they could do to support an ambitious agenda of change. The opportunity here was to provide these people with assignments and projects that stretched them and moved us closer to Cathy's vision for the company. To be honest, the leadership challenge here is to define the desired outcome and then just get out of the way. Leadership is a lot easier when you have talented and motivated people working on your team.

If you have led major change efforts in your career, it won't surprise you to learn that my team also had a large number of folks who thought things had been just fine and were not interested in changing the way they approached their work. They were not bad people, but no amount of persuasion from Cathy or me was going to get them excited about doing their work differently. My mistake was in waiting too long to make the changes needed in the makeup of the team. I wanted to give everyone a fair shot to succeed but extended the wait period too long. What happened to me was what Ed Sannini of Morgan Stanley has experienced in his career and has observed with other executives. In talking about the importance of getting the right people on the team, Sannini says,

You have to have the right people reporting to you because you can't back them up. If it is not the right person, you have to take them out and replace them or else you are going to be doing their role and you can't do that at an executive level. Implicit in moving to that next level is that you trust that the people under you can do it. If they can't do it, either you can't move up or you are going to be straddling both levels.

The dilemma that I fell into was straddling both levels. Because my total team was not prepared to implement the change agenda and still deliver the basic functions of an HR department, I found myself stretched too thin between ensuring that things were done and done well in my department and participating and contributing fully to the work of the executive team. I could not do the latter until I had put the right people in place to take care of the former.

Asking people who are not a good fit to leave your team is one of the toughest things that you have to do as an executive. As one of my colleagues once said in a senior staff meeting, "If letting people go doesn't keep you up at night, then you're not taking it seriously enough." In spite of the difficulty of it, you have to do it when necessary. In research conducted for *Right from the Start,* Dan Ciampa and Michael Watkins report that not making key personnel changes soon enough is one of the most frequently cited mistakes that new executives recall when asked to assess their own performance in their roles. Lucien Alziari offers this advice on how to think about and work through the process of letting go of people who don't fit the needs of the team and the organization:

What I see is that a lot of people . . . try to do their best with the people they have. And I always ask them the question, "Do you think you've got the right people in the first place?" That becomes a fairly definitive question. I think it is a real rite of passage for leaders to . . . have that kind of detachment to look at the team in an objective way and to say, "I know them, I love them, I really want them to do well, I want the best for them, but the bottom line is, Can they deliver what is needed by the organization?" That is really what it is all about. . . . If I've got time and think they are going to get there, I would always stick with the players I have. But you have to be very objective in answering that question.

## Redefine How You Add Value

Having the right people in the right roles on your functional team creates the opportunity for you to redefine how you add value to the work of the team and the goals of the organization as a whole. Many of the executives that I have either coached or interviewed have spoken of the shift that they have had to make in how they add value to the organization. As individual contributors or functional team leaders, they added value by actually creating or doing something. It might have been conducting a financial analysis, closing a key sale, or determining how to improve a production process. The line of sight between what they did and the result they achieved was tangible and clear. As executives, they have learned that their value-added is more intangible. More often than not, their value is in either facilitating or interpreting the work of others. The facilitation of the work often involves using executive influence to secure needed resources or to lower barriers to getting important work done. Sometimes the facilitation of the work comes by adding a perspective that is not available to your team but is to you as an executive.

As an executive, you have access to broader perspectives that can add value through the way you direct, interpret, and present the work of your team. Your role is not to check the work for accuracy (you should have the right people in place to do that) but to frame its broader implications for the organization. Ed Sannini first hit the executive level about ten years ago when he moved to Tokyo to lead the audit function for JP Morgan's businesses in Asia. Thinking back to that transition, Sannini remembers this as the basic change he made as an executive: "I was no longer making sure the audit reports were correct, but I was taking the results of those and providing a value-added. My value-added was in taking those reports that were handed to me and bringing [their conclusions] to another level versus confirming that what was handed to me was correct and letting someone else interpret it."

Making such a shift in how you add value can be difficult if your style has been to dig into the details to ensure that everything is done perfectly. To make this shift, you will need to learn to determine when good enough is good enough. A number of years ago, economist Arthur Okun described this as knowing when to optimize and when to *satisfice*. In his analysis, few initiatives really require an optimal solution. In most cases, a satisfactory solution is good enough. The best decision makers, he found, are those who know when the optimal solution is required and when, as is most often the case, a satisfactory solution will suffice (hence, his word *satisfice*).

Steve Linehan, senior vice president and treasurer of Capital One, made some strong points about the challenges he had in his career around learning to satisfice and the difference learning to do so made in his capacity to add value as an executive. His story started when he was promoted to an executive role at the Federal Deposit Insurance Corporation (FDIC) and continued at Capital One. His experience relates directly to the discussion earlier in this chapter about getting your ego out of the way by letting go of the work:

> You know, the pick up/let go thing really hit me hard at the FDIC. I was very much a control freak. . . . There were certain ways that I learned how to do things in terms of the quality and thoroughness of work, how to write things, and I was put in a role where you just couldn't do that. You were really forced to let go. It's almost like an alcoholic admitting he is an alcoholic. You get to a point to where you can't do it. You simply can't.

So I began to delegate work and I think the biggest thing for me was accepting work that was really good. It might not have been the way I would have done it, but it was really, really good. Accepting that was incredibly liberating. From that point on I think I began to accelerate.

Linehan's success at the FDIC led to employment at Capital One, where he reached the executive level soon after his arrival at the company. Because he was in a different environment, Linehan had to continue to learn to adjust and make changes in the way he added value to the work. A big shift involved learning to focus on outcomes rather than on the details of doing the work:

I was working my butt off, and there were a lot of late nights and producing a lot of work, [but] my performance review wasn't that great. It wasn't commensurate with . . . the effort I was putting in. The tough love there was that I had to stop doing what I was doing in terms of doing it all, doing all the work myself. I had to really focus on getting other people to do the work. It was doing more . . . of getting people aligned or [getting people] from other groups to align behind what I wanted to do . . . and doing less of the on-the-fly preparation. I was doing it all on the fly, because . . . I was caught in the mindset, as many leaders are, of, "It will take me longer to teach somebody else how to do it than for me to do it myself." I was completely caught in that mode, but it didn't get me anything at the end of the day. . . . It didn't meet the expectations of my boss. It wasn't what he wanted me to do.

To deliver the results his boss expected, Linehan says, he realized that he needed to rely on "the 80/20 rule." Linehan described it as identifying what quality of work from the team is good enough to get the desired outcome: "That's what it is all about anyway, getting the outcomes you want." In my experience, a good application of the 80/20 rule is to assess which 20 percent of your efforts will yield 80 percent of the desired results. From the perspective of your role as an executive, the 20 percent of your effort is in clearly defining the desired outcome and making sure that it is well understood by your team. We will cover that in more detail in Chapter 6, in the context of picking up the practice of defining what to do and letting go of telling how to do it. For now, I want to share with you a question that I encourage my clients to ask themselves when they need to think through the most powerful ways in which they can add value. The question, which I hope you will regularly ask yourself, is this:

> *What is it, that—given the perspective and resources*
> *I have as an executive—only I can do?*

The list of answers to that question should be short but high in value-added. Everything else that is not on the list, but is still important, should be handled by your team or someone else's team.

## Build and Lead So That the Team Is Actually a Team

When coaching leaders and their teams, I often use a planning tool called GRPI, which was developed at General Electric. GRPI is an acronym that stands for

- Goals

- Roles and Responsibilities

- Plans and Processes

- Interpersonal Norms

I especially like the GRPI model because it highlights the elements that need to be clear for a team to practice real teamwork. The goals describe the outcomes that define success for the team. The roles and responsibilities, and how they overlap and intersect, need to be clear for each team member. Attention to plans and processes helps clarify critical success factors and leads to the creation of a game plan with clear tasks, a schedule with milestones, and measures of success. Finally, the interpersonal norms describe the team's operating agreements and the behaviors that are required for team effectiveness. While each GRPI element is essential to team success, the executives I interviewed about team reliance emphasized the importance of establishing and following through on ground rules that build effective teamwork. In quick-hit fashion, here are some of their best ideas for how to do that:

- *Get the team involved in shaping goals:* Lucien Alziari describes this as the process of "getting the team involved in where we are going." He explains, "[Talking through] 'What is it that we collectively have as our mission and strategies for the next three to five years?' is really important because then you are really engaging people at a much more personal and emotional level."

- *Encourage team problem solving:* An important lesson learned by Donna Morea of CGI-AMS has been to give her team the space to work with each other in solving problems and resolving disagreements. Morea notes that leaders sometimes show "a tendency when a couple of people go at it to say, 'OK, let's take this off-line.'" Donna learned the importance of not doing this early in her executive career when one of her directs asked her to give the team space to learn to resolve conflicts constructively rather than sweeping them under the rug only to have them reappear another day.

- *Cultivate a diversity of views:* Mark Stavish told me that when he was with AOL, one of his objectives for his team was "to facilitate some kind of constructive disagreement, diversity of opinion, [and] diversity of talent. . . . You need some of those contrarians in the organization to keep you honest," Stavish says. He found that having and drawing out a real diversity of experience and perspective on the team led to better results for the business. Mary Good, a senior vice president of Blackboard, an education enterprise software provider, agrees with Stavish and adds, "People who are different actually come up with ideas that are better than yours in many cases. Part of your value as an executive is leveraging the talent of other people. It's not just about you."

- *Promote honest feedback:* When soliciting feedback for my executive clients, I sometimes hear that they could be more effective if they were perceived as being more approachable. If they send signals that they are not open to feedback, they won't hear what they need to hear from their team. To build a highly effective team, it is important to create an environment in which feedback is both solicited and offered. Mary Good says that when she became an executive, "I looked for people who would give me honest feedback and were not afraid to get in my face if they disagreed with me. So that's the number one thing I was looking for . . . people that would have the chutzpah and the assertiveness and the confidence to tell me the emperor has no clothes."

- *Show respect and earn trust:* As I noted in Chapter 4, presence begets presence. This is especially true when it comes to leaders and their teams. The presence that you present to the team is predictive of what you will receive in return. As Stephen Cerrone of JP Morgan Chase says, "It is virtually impossible to be successful as a leader unless you have followers. The only way you are going to have followers is if you treat them with respect and they trust you about what you are doing." Linguist and management consultant Fernando Flores believes that trust is based on three factors: sincerity, credibility, and competence. As an executive picking up team reliance and letting go of self-reliance, these are characteristics you should strive to project yourself and to expect from the members of your team.

(10 **TIPS**)   **For Picking Up Team Reliance
and Letting Go of Self-Reliance**

1   Ask trusted colleagues for feedback on strengths that will serve you well as an executive—and the strengths that you will need to tone down.

2   Train your ego to derive satisfaction from what your team accomplishes, not from what you accomplish.

3   Spend your energy enabling your team, not competing with them.

4   Quickly build a team that gets results. Otherwise, the pace at the next level will be too fast for you to keep up.

5   In assessing your team, honestly ask yourself, "Do I have the right people in the first place?" If the answer is no, make changes quickly but with respect and compassion.

6   Increase your value-added by structuring the work of your team through the lens of your executive perspective.

7   In working with your team, focus on defining the desired outcome and making sure it is well understood.

8   When delegating to your team, begin with a clear and realistic assessment of what "good enough" looks like.

9   To check your value-added, regularly ask yourself, "What is it that—given the perspective and resources I have as an executive—only I can do?"

10   Use the GRPI model to build an effective team. Establish the interpersonal norms that separate great teams from good teams.

## 6

- ## PICK UP DEFINING WHAT TO DO

- ## LET GO OF TELLING HOW TO DO IT

As you make the shift from self-reliance to team reliance, you'll notice that one of the biggest obstacles to overcome is letting go of telling your team how to do the work. The likely reason that you have been designated an executive is that you have demonstrated throughout your career an ability to get things done in a particular functional discipline. You have shown again and again that you are an expert in how to accomplish something and you have been recognized and rewarded for that expertise. As you moved into leadership roles you may have let go of some of your workload and turned it over to your team. You have probably still been spending a lot of time, however, explaining to your team how to do the work. Up to a point, this is appropriate. By sharing what you know with your team members, you are developing them and building their capacity to contribute to the organization. At what point, however, does your willingness, even eagerness, to tell the team how to do the work become too much? If you are an executive, or soon will be, you have reached that point. Instead of telling your team how to do the work, you now need to define the work your team needs to do.

Letting go of telling your team how to do the work will test your comfort level. You know your discipline better than most. You have gotten where you are because you are very, very good at something. It's no wonder that you're comfortable with it, and the idea of turning over the nuts and bolts of the operation is unsettling.

I've known many executives over the years who could not let go of the details for fear that something would go wrong or that the work would not be done in the way they thought best. The results for these people, their teams, and their organizations were always less than expected. An executive who constantly tells the team how to do the work is stretched too thin to be effective and is also not paying proper attention to the real work of the next level. Teams who work for executives like this stagnate rather than grow. Organizations with too many such executives don't achieve as much as they should. In talking with me, former AOL executive Mark Stavish shared a great line that addresses how executives should view their role. Mark told me that in executive team meetings, chief operating officer Bob Pittman would remind his colleagues that they were "the keepers of the what, not the masters of the how."

## A Focus on "What" Requires the Right People

By focusing on what rather than how, you will be playing in the realm of the strategic rather than the tactical. To do this fully, you will, of course, have to have the right team in place. Having the right people in the right roles is not only the prerequisite to team reliance, it is also the key factor that will enable you to get comfortable in picking up defining what to do and letting go of telling how to do it.

Steve Rippe, a retired major general in the U.S. Army, is currently COO of the Protestant Episcopal Cathedral Foundation. In that role, Rippe oversees the operations of the National Cathedral in Washington, D.C., as well as the private schools and other entities associated with the Cathedral. After a twenty-nine-year career in the Army, Rippe has learned the value of having capable people in place who can determine how to do the work based on a definition of what to do.

Rippe told me that, a few months after he arrived at the Cathedral Foundation, he concluded that the organization needed a viable plan for conducting a state funeral. Given his experience in the Army, Rippe was capable of creating such a plan himself, but he recognized that the scope of his role as COO required that his attention be spread more broadly. Rippe hired a retired lieutenant colonel who had worked for him in the Army and was an expert in project planning. Rippe recruited him to join the Foundation staff as director of operations. His new hire's first priority was to update the Cathedral's plan for conducting a state funeral.

Some months later, his director of operations delivered to Rippe a thick, color-coded loose-leaf binder with a complete plan for conducting such an event. A few weeks after that, Rippe was having a drink with his wife on a Saturday afternoon at Washington's Mayflower Hotel when his cell phone rang. The Episcopal bishop of Washington was calling to say that he had just received word that former President Reagan had died. In relating the story to me, Rippe recalled that the bishop asked him if they should meet immediately at the Cathedral to plan the funeral. Knowing that the plan was already complete, Rippe suggested that they meet early the next morning instead. On Sunday before mass, Rippe and his staff met with the bishop to go over the plan and then disassembled the binder and spread its contents on a wall in the office to use as a master schedule for the upcoming week.

As anyone who watched the Reagan funeral events unfold on television knows, everything from the Reagan family's arrival in

Washington to their departure a few days later for the burial in California went flawlessly. I asked Rippe if he had gotten much sleep that week. He said that, with the exception of the night before the funeral, it was a normal week in terms of the hours he kept. On the morning of the funeral, Rippe and his staff arrived at the Cathedral around 4:00 A.M. to work with the television networks setting up cameras and lighting. As soon as the funeral was over, the Cathedral team reset the building for a previously scheduled high school graduation ceremony at 2:00 P.M. and then once again for a wedding rehearsal in the Cathedral that evening. Several months before, Steve Rippe had defined what to do. His highly capable staff had come up with a brilliant plan for how to do it. The world saw the results of their work during the week of President Reagan's funeral.

## Allow Your Team to Determine "How"

By rising to the rank of major general in the U.S. Army, Steve Rippe demonstrated his strength in operational planning and execution. Did President Reagan's funeral go exactly the way it would have if Rippe had planned it himself? Probably not. Did it go exceedingly well anyway? Absolutely. That was the outcome that he had in mind when he put the right team in place and then defined for them what to do. When you are an expert or accomplished in a particular field, it can be difficult to let go of offering your opinions or direction on how to carry out a project. To play at the right level as an executive, however, you have to learn how to let go.

This is a lesson that George Sterner, vice president of strategic pursuits for Raytheon Corporation, learned as an officer in the U.S. Navy. While he retired as a vice admiral and commander of Naval Sea Systems Command, a 90,000-person organization with fifty-two locations worldwide, Sterner began his career as a naval officer under the command of Admiral Hyman Rickover, father of the nuclear navy. Rickover, who served on active duty until he was eighty, was a brilliant perfectionist and notorious taskmaster. To serve successfully under him, you had to know your stuff, and George Sterner did. Talking about his leadership lessons, Sterner said, "In certain aspects of engineering, I'm an expert. I most likely know the right answer. I learned, though, that knowing the right answer is not always the most important thing." After he had commanded a nuclear submarine, Sterner led a team that inspected subs. Sterner recalls, "I went from commanding one submarine to now looking at forty different ones a year for up to thirty hours each. . . . I realized that, and this was the biggest eye-opener for me, there are hundreds of different ways of running those submarines. And a lot of them turned out pretty well. It was just not the way I did it. That was a big lesson."

It's probably a fortunate thing for the world that most of us aren't charged with leading a team that runs a nuclear submarine. Sterner's story provides a good perspective check that there is often more than one way to achieve a desired outcome. Having grown up professionally under one of history's great perfectionists, George Sterner deserves a lot of credit for letting go of telling how to do the work and focusing instead on defining successful outcomes. Mary Good of Blackboard has seen the same dynamic in her private sector career. Good says, "One of the most important things to let go of is being a perfectionist. . . . You shouldn't give up on the drive or the intensity, but you have to give up on the perfectionism from the standpoint that just because someone who works for you doesn't do it exactly the same way you would, as long as the goal and the results are in line with the strategy that you set, you have to let them do it their way."

Even at the executive level, it may seem that there are times when you need to get involved with your team in determining how the work is done. How do you know if your sense that you should get involved is legitimate or just a sign that you have more work to do in learning to let go of telling the team how to do it?

Jason Jeffay of Hewitt Associates offers some questions to consider when you are thinking through the appropriate depth of your involvement in the how: "The questions that you should be asking yourself are not 'Can I do something good here or can I produce a good outcome?' [Instead, the right question is,] 'By spending my time on this activity or this process, do I produce a better result for the total group?'"

If the answer is yes, get involved. If it's no, back off. However, if you find yourself answering yes to this question most of the time, you either need to adjust your perspective of where and how you should be making your best contributions or you need to raise the quality of your team. It is that simple. Your job as an executive is, as Bob Pittman said, to be a keeper of the what, not a master of the how.

## Get Clear on the Big Picture

Pittman's distinction around what and how has an important implication. As a member of the executive team, you are *a* keeper of the what, but not *the* keeper of the what. Partner with your executive colleagues to determine what is most important to the big-picture strategy of the organization and then determine what contribution your part of the organization must make to that strategy. Of all your executive colleagues, your boss will probably be your most important source for determining what you need to do. Drawing on career experience that led to the position of CEO of Budget Rent A Car, Bill Plamondon offers this advice on how new executives should seek clarity about what they should be contributing:

> What works . . . [is when] the organization is clear. If you go into a new area or a new job . . . the one thing that helps you get a better perspective is to ask your immediate boss, 'What is the job description? What are the responsibilities? . . . Describe for me, in writing if you can, what the objectives are.

What are the behaviors that you think are appropriate?' The more clarity you can get, the more it allows you to make that change successfully. . . . [The key questions are,] 'What is the role? What are the responsibilities? What are the accountabilities? And, what is success and what are the metrics to understand that?' . . . [The point of all this is not that . . . ] your job is [to do] these tasks, . . . but rather to ensure that your people do these tasks well and on time.

There may be times in your executive career when you have a manager who will not be as explicit in defining success as Bill Plamondon was for his executives. In such cases, it makes sense to follow advice that Steve Rippe learned in his career as an Army officer. Rippe found, as he moved through the ranks, especially at the level of colonel (the Army's equivalent to an entry-level executive position) and above, that it became more and more important to look at what he and his soldiers were expected to deliver through the eyes of his boss.

To do this, assume the perspective of your boss and ask yourself three questions:

- What do I think about this?

- How do I feel about this?

- What do I want from this?

Tim Gallwey calls the process of assuming the perspective of another person *transposing*. To develop the empathy needed to understand the other person's perspective, it is important to ask the questions in the first person (What do *I* want?) and not the third person (What does *he* want?). Once you have developed a sense of what your boss wants, check it out in direct conversation or talk with trusted executive colleagues who understand the bigger picture.

Whether you get clarity on what to do directly from your boss or indirectly through other means, it is important to get it so that you can lead your functional team effectively. Tim Gallwey has developed a simple acronym, STOP:

**S**tep back

**T**hink

**O**rganize your thoughts

**P**roceed

This is a good process to practice regularly and is particularly important to do as you determine what is most important for your team to accomplish. As Lucien Alziari of Avon says, "[The executives] who really elevate themselves . . . figure out at the strategic level where they are trying to go and then just coach people to get to the right place in terms of their own individual contributions."

## Understanding "What," Driving "How"

As Alziari suggests, once you have developed clarity for yourself about what needs to be accomplished in support of the bigger picture, your next responsibility as an executive is to share your understanding of what to do with your team and then ensure that excellent execution occurs. It should be no surprise that the first step in driving successful execution is to have the right people on your team. There is no substitute for having high-quality talent applied to the work. If you don't yet have the right team, develop your people quickly or recruit new people who can meet the demands of the work.

Assuming that your team is capable and reliable, the next most important step in driving excellent execution is to make sure that you are clear on what you want your people to achieve and that they understand the direction and their responsibilities in achieving results. A number of our executive mentors have offered their most successful methods for establishing clarity around what to do and developing comfort around how it is done:

- Perspective transference

- Setting expectations

- Establishing guidelines and systems

- Selecting levers of control

Some or all of these methods may work for you. What follows is a brief description of each method.

## Perspective Transference

For Mike Lanier of Verizon, the process of fully communicating what to do reminds him of the team-building game in which every member of the team is blindfolded except the one who is selected to give the rest of the team directions on moving from point A to point B. Lanier's experience with the game is that the instruction giver has to be specific and regularly check for understanding to ensure that the team gets it in terms of direction. He has found that it is important for him to be equally explicit with his team in defining what needs to be accomplished.

When he reached the executive level, Lanier learned that one of the most valuable resources he can bring to his team is the perspective and insight that he gets from participating in meetings with other executives. His team members do not have the opportunity to get that perspective from anyone other than Lanier. I call this dynamic *perspective transference*. If Mike Lanier does not take the opportunity to transfer his perspective to his team when defining what needs to be done, he may as well not have it in the first place. The power of executive level perspective and insight is in how it is used to shape direction and drive action through team members. It has no other purpose. By sharing your perspective with your team, you not only deepen their understanding of what to do, you build their motivation and commitment by helping them understand the why behind the what.

## Setting Expectations

Setting expectations with your team should focus on both the what and the how. Earlier, Bill Plamondon talked about the importance of being clear about what to do by taking time to learn and define what success looks like. This is a critical conversation to have with your team. At the outset of a major project or initiative, everyone needs to have the same answers to the questions that define success. These are some of the questions that should be asked and answered in such a conversation:

- When we're successful, what will be different from today's status quo?

- What difference will success make?

- What are the metrics that will help us to measure success?

- On the way to achieving the desired result, what actions are out of bounds?

- What is our deadline?

Once expectations are clear about what to do, it is important to take some time with your team to set expectations about how you want to be involved in the work. As an executive, you will find that time and attention are two of your most precious commodities. It is essential, therefore, to establish clarity with your team on when they should bring you into the stream of work and ask for your perspective and assistance. Steve Linehan of Capital One has thought a lot about this process and offers this approach, which may work for you as well:

I establish expectations about what the quality of work should be that reaches my desk. That helps define for my team what it is they need to bring me in on. . . . If you set out those expectations, I think it gives people frameworks for when to bring you in. [I want the team to think,] "We ought to bring Steve in when we have a well-thought-out point of view or recommendation."

I don't want them bringing me in when they're brainstorming, . . . or when the ideas aren't very well formed. . . . I expect them to come in with a point of view. A lot of times when people are not sure, they will want you to get involved in solving the problems with them. . . . You don't have time to do it anymore. I can't be engaged in problem solving. That's what I need the team to do. I'm happy to have them bounce a question off me from time to time but I'm not going to sit down and problem solve. . . . There are too many issues to deal with them all one on one.

So, if you set expectations high enough for quality work, then I think that sends a message to the team on what is expected and when they need to bring you in. I really only want to see something that is well thought out. [The team's checkpoint for when to bring me in should be when they say,] "Steve can bring a broader perspective because he probably knows some things from his conversations with his peers that we don't."

Linehan touches on a couple of important points in his comments. First, he is clear that he expects the team to do its own high-quality problem solving after he has worked with the group to define the desired outcome. Second, when the team does bring him in during the problem-solving process, he expects that to generally be for the purposes of the perspective transference that I talked about earlier. By following this approach, Linehan leverages the resources available to him as an executive for the benefit of his team, himself, and the organization as a whole.

## Establishing Guidelines and Systems

In Chapter 7, we'll deal in depth with the importance of setting up systems for monitoring the work that drives results. As a quick preview of that discussion, I want to share some additional perspective from George Sterner on the practice of defining what to do and how to follow up on progress:

> I think it is incumbent on leaders to set guidelines for the results and get out of the way. . . . But it's also important to set up your own systems with your team to check on how things are going. You certainly don't want to be a hands-off manager. You don't want to sit there in your office. You've got to get out.

Sterner's approach may come across as more hands-on than Steve Linehan's. It's important to recognize, though, that they both agree on the need to define results and get out of the way. An important part of Sterner's leadership style is to establish open communications by staying visible. To support that style, his systems for following up rely heavily on being available in informal settings. Linehan's style is also to be available to his team, but he places more emphasis on the conditions for when he wants to be brought into the conversation. Neither approach is right or wrong; they depend on the style of the executive and the culture of the organization. The common denominators in both approaches are setting guidelines for defining what the team should accomplish and providing an appropriate degree of availability to follow up on how progress is being made.

## Selecting Levers of Control

Understanding how to give up control and what sort of control to give up is a challenge that most new executives have to work through. The theme of this chapter provides guidance on how to strike the right balance in selecting which levers you should control. As an executive leader, you need to maintain a stronger measure of control and influence around what needs to be done. As George Sterner and others have counseled, it is advisable for you to give up more control around how the work gets done.

Hewitt's Jason Jeffay shared a nice metaphor with me in describing the levers of control that he uses in keeping a project on track. In thinking about his role as an executive leader, Jeffay says,

> I often visualize my job as nudging the boat. You know, the boat is going down a particular path and I have the opportunity to exert influence, sort of nudge the boat to the left or right, to try to get it someplace where I think it can go or nudge it again to get it to go a little bit farther.
>
> To me, the first key mechanism for doing this is goals, making sure you are crystal clear on what you want your people to be doing and what you are going to hold them accountable for. . . . And then the second is standards. How high is high? Standards and goals are two of the key levers that you can use to make sure that the total organization you are responsible for is going down the right path at the right speed.

Jeffay's metaphor focuses on maintaining the correct direction and speed of the boat, not how to make the engine run as fast as it can. His chosen levers of control place the emphasis on what to do, not how to do it. Doing this allows both Jeffay and his team to operate at the right level.

## "What" Builds Next-Level Capacity

As an executive, you'll be responsible for identifying and developing individuals who have the capacity to move to the next level themselves. By picking up defining what to do and letting go of telling how to do it, you are taking an important step in developing those people as future leaders of your organization, which is one of your primary new responsibilities. In research conducted for *High Flyers* and other works, University of Southern California professor of management and organization Morgan McCall has found that high-potential leaders develop more fully and quickly through on-the-job experience than by any other method. The way you lead your team can have a huge impact on their professional development.

In our interviews, one executive after another spoke about the importance of allowing good people the space to develop by doing the work in the ways that they think are best. Mary Good said that she learned an important lesson as she developed as an executive: "You have to appreciate that people work differently, and if you aren't able to do that you stifle people and you are not going to get the best out of them." Steve Linehan talked with me about giving people the freedom to make more decisions and said that, for an executive, it is important to learn not to "let little things get you wrapped around an axle." On the way to getting the work done, it won't all be done in the way you would do it. But if it gets done in a way that leads to a good and timely outcome, that can be more than enough, especially when you consider the positive effects of developmental experience for your team and creating more time for you to play at the next level.

From his vantage point as a senior HR executive in two very successful Fortune 500 companies, Lucien Alziari offers this perspective on what can happen for executives and their teams when they play the right roles in defining what to do and determining how to do it:

> One of the real tests for me is, if you look at the vice president and their team, is everybody playing at the right level or, ideally, are they playing at the next level? With the teams that get it wrong, everybody is playing a level down. They are too down into the details. They are doing the subordinates' jobs because the subordinates are doing *their* subordinates' jobs. You really are not doing what the organization needs you to do. But when it's really working as it should, you are doing your boss's job and they love you for it.

Alziari's comments paint a clear picture of what it looks like when everyone is operating with the comfort and confidence that come from knowing they are performing at their best. As a leader moving to the next level, you have the wonderful opportunity not only to grow and develop yourself but to guide others on the journey of advancing through the uncharted terrain of their next level.

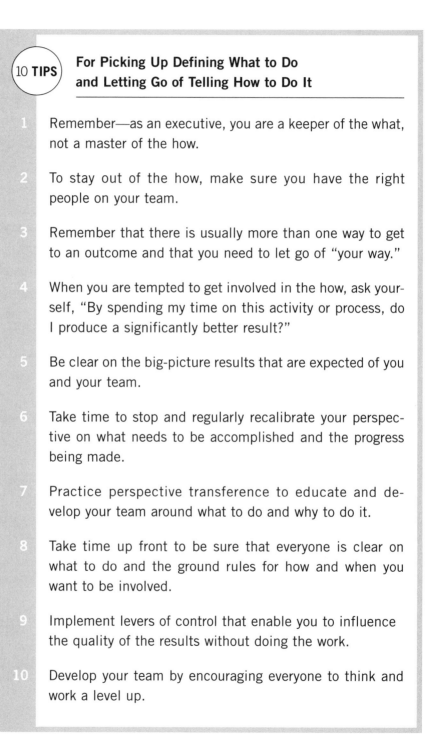

**10 TIPS** For Picking Up Defining What to Do
and Letting Go of Telling How to Do It

1. Remember—as an executive, you are a keeper of the what,
not a master of the how.

2. To stay out of the how, make sure you have the right
people on your team.

3. Remember that there is usually more than one way to get
to an outcome and that you need to let go of "your way."

4. When you are tempted to get involved in the how, ask yourself, "By spending my time on this activity or process, do
I produce a significantly better result?"

5. Be clear on the big-picture results that are expected of you
and your team.

6. Take time to stop and regularly recalibrate your perspective on what needs to be accomplished and the progress
being made.

7. Practice perspective transference to educate and develop your team around what to do and why to do it.

8. Take time up front to be sure that everyone is clear on
what to do and the ground rules for how and when you
want to be involved.

9. Implement levers of control that enable you to influence
the quality of the results without doing the work.

10. Develop your team by encouraging everyone to think and
work a level up.

# 7

# PICK UP ACCOUNTABILITY FOR MANY RESULTS

## LET GO OF RESPONSIBILITY FOR A FEW RESULTS

I first heard the distinction between accountability and responsibility several years ago when I was conducting a feedback interview for a client with his senior executive boss. In talking about the development opportunities for my client, the executive said, "He needs to make the shift from being responsible for a few things to being accountable for a lot of things." When I asked the executive to say more about this, he said that by holding on to a responsibility mindset, my client was limiting himself to a playing field that was too small for his capabilities.

This distinction between responsibility and accountability turns on who is actually doing the work and how work is defined. In the responsibility model, you are the person who either does the work or closely monitors others who are doing the work. If you are responsible, you are likely to step in and do chunks of the work from time to time. You may even be doing chunks of the work all of the time. Either way, you're almost certainly going to personally make sure that the work comes together well and that it leads to the desired result. Because of the personal attention that the responsibility model requires, a leader can successfully manage only one or just a few results. There is nothing wrong with the responsibility model. Organizations need managers who are effective at operating in this space.

Successful executives learn to shift from being responsible to being accountable. In the accountability model, you are accountable for—you answer for—the results that others are responsible for achieving. The accountability model brings together the key elements of the two preceding distinctions around what to pick up and let go to be a successful executive. First, you have to pick up team reliance and let go of self-reliance. It's probably obvious that the accountability model will not work for you as an executive leader if you don't have a strong team that you trust and can rely on. Next, you have to pick up defining what to do and let go of telling how to do it. The executive leader who successfully picks up accountability for many results is focused on outcomes. Outcomes begin with a clear definition of what to do. Executives who work from the accountability model are defining what to do across a range of issues, applying a perspective that is at a higher level and has a longer-term focus than those of their reporting managers. Their job is to set the agenda and bring the different streams of work together in a way that supports not just their own agenda but also the larger organization's agenda. They are accountable for the results that support the agenda. The reporting managers and their teams are responsible for delivering those results.

In this chapter, we'll spend some time digging into the behaviors and mind-sets that you'll need to adopt to make the shift from being responsible to being accountable. Let's start by looking at how successful executives define work.

## Reframe Your Definition of Work

If you're like me, you either are or know someone who enjoys mowing their lawn. Most people derive a real sense of satisfaction from setting out to do something and, in a relatively short time, completing it. When you cut your grass, you can stand back and look at it and know that you did the work. There is no ambiguity around the results. You cut the grass.

You've probably had that same sensation in your career at different times. You wrote an analysis or a report. You negotiated an important deal. You closed a big sale. You implemented a new process or led a complex project. In any of these cases, you knew when the work was done and, on most days, you could probably leave for home with a sense of clarity about what you accomplished over the past several hours.

When you operate at the executive level, you face a more intangible and ambiguous definition of what you accomplish on any given day. To be successful, you're going to have to stop the corporate equivalent of cutting the grass yourself and instead hire a lawn service. Your satisfaction will need to come from the fact that the grass got cut, not that you did it yourself. To extend the analogy a little further, you need to start thinking of yourself as the owner of a lawn care business dealing with a hundred yards a week. There is no way you're going to cut all that grass yourself; you're going to rely on your yard crews to cut the grass. Your work is to oversee the process, stay accountable to your customers, and begin planning your extension into the landscaping business. You're probably not going to go home at the end of the day with grass stains on your shoes and smelling a little bit like gasoline. That doesn't mean, though, that you didn't do any work during the day. You did—you just can't touch the result.

Before you conclude that my lawn-mowing analogy is a bit tortured, let me tell you that I've worked with dozens of executives who have had a hard time letting go of whatever their version is of cutting the grass themselves. Recently, I was with a new client, a brilliant scientist who, at the vice president level, has moved from doing research himself to leading several teams responsible for research and development. He told me in our last meeting that he feels a bit unsettled because he often asks himself on the drive home, "What did I do all day?" Instead of working in the lab, he's working in meetings about what the people in the lab are doing.

Like George Sterner of Raytheon, my client is an expert in his field and most likely knows the right answer to a particular research question. In terms of day-to-day implementation, that doesn't matter. My client is accountable for the results of several teams. Each team is responsible for its specific results. The challenge for my client is to develop a new understanding and appreciation for the work he does every day. He is learning how to operate in the accountability model and move away from the comfort and familiarity of the responsibility model. The nature of his work has changed.

## Letting Go of the Responsibility Model

One of the primary themes of this book is that personal transformation is required to operate successfully at the executive level. Much of that transformative process is in learning to become comfortable leaving behind old skills and behaviors that served you well earlier in your career or maybe in your life. Most of us have heard all of our lives (especially from our parents!) that we need to be responsible. I'm not arguing against personal responsibility for executives. Far from it. One could make a strong argument that just about every corporate scandal over the past several years, from Enron to Tyco, stemmed from an absence of personal responsibility. In the sense that responsibility equates to ethics and a moral compass, I am all for it. I don't think you can be a successful executive or human being without it.

The point I am making, though, is that, as an executive, you have to let go of personal responsibility for every outcome. Henry Lucas is CEO and co-founder of Engineering Consulting Services (ECS), a privately held firm that has grown in the past twenty years from one office in Northern Virginia to twenty-four offices with seven hundred employees across the United States. ECS is recognized as a leader in its field and has consulted on such projects as FedEx Field and the headquarters of the World Bank and America Online. As someone who has grown over the course of his career from an engineer to a bootstrap entrepreneur to the leader of a multimillion-dollar company, Henry has thought a lot about the changes he has had to make to keep himself and his company operating at the right level. He has this to say about his need to let go of the responsibility model of management:

> I am an engineer and I enjoy engineering. As the company grew and I took on a broader leadership role, I found myself getting dragged back into day-to-day issues probably more than I should have. That's probably the toughest thing. I mean at one point you wake up and realize that you have to stop being what you were at the beginning of your career and become something else. It is a very difficult thing to do for most people, I would say. Some people obviously are better at it than others. But I think if you have a real passion for what you do for a living, there is a certain part of you that doesn't want to give that up. And yet to go to the next level, that's exactly what you have to do—and then hopefully you will have a passion for what the next level of activity is. And if you do, you will be very successful in that as well.

One of the more interesting points that Henry makes is that, as you move to the next level, your passion needs to shift from a narrow focus to a broad focus. You could argue that making this shift is at the essence of what it takes to make the shift from functional manager to executive leader. Henry Lucas describes what that shift looks like in the context of his engineering consulting company:

> You need to transition from being a doer to a manager to a leader. The biggest difference between a manager and a leader is that the manager needs to know and, in fact, should have more details about the day-to-day operations. They should have a much stronger handle on it. They are asking questions like: What report needs to go out this week? Who needs to be contacted? Which clients are a little unhappy with what we have done or which clients are very happy with what we have done and could recommend us for other things? [The questions and focus are around] the nuts and bolts of the operation.
>
> The leader has to have a broader view. He or she is going to know less about the day-to-day operations but should know more about the strategic opportunities that are out there. Where is the market heading? Do we want to be in this particular sector of work? Where do we want to open up offices? Why do we want to open up offices? And I think, lastly, a leader also needs to be more in tune with the whole recruiting process.

Notice the difference in the questions that Lucas describes for a leader as opposed to a manager. The manager's questions focus on the day-to-day responsibilities of management reporting, customer satisfaction, and new business development. In contrast, the leader's questions focus on the strategies of the competitive positioning of the company, options for expansion, and acquiring the talent needed to expand. The beauty of this comparison is that in a well-functioning organization such as ECS, all the important work gets done. The responsibility for results is clear. It rests with the functional managers. The accountability for results is also clear. It rests with the executive leaders.

## The Implications of the Accountability Model

Changing your view of how you contribute to the work getting done may feel like a leap of faith. Indeed, you will be relying on no more than faith unless you think strategically and systematically about how to make and successfully sustain this change. The accountability model of executive leadership has three implications that I want to draw your attention to:

- "What have you done for me lately?" becomes a more frequent question.

- You own the results for good or for bad.

- You and your peers are accountable for solving bigger problems.

Let's take some time to dig deeper into each of these implications.

### What Have You Done for Me Lately?

Steve Smith is senior vice president and treasurer of American Electric Power. Still in his early forties, Smith has been a senior executive in two other companies besides AEP. He has made the executive transition a number of times in his career and notes, "Once you become a vice president you are viewed in a different light. That light is as somebody who has to think broadly and as somebody who has to get things done." In the context of being expected to get things done, Ed Sannini of Morgan Stanley described one of the most challenging lessons he had to learn when he first became an executive: "Your value is on what you brought to the table that day. The executive level view is, 'What have you done for me lately?' It is not what have you done over the last two years, three years, five years, or fifteen years. As an executive, you are assessed much more on a shorter-term cycle."

Mike Lanier noticed this dynamic when he moved up to the executive level at Verizon. He notes,

> [At the executive level, you have] clear accountability, whereas before you were one of many people who had your hands in the stuff. There were some projects that you had more accountability for but you always had your executive who carried the brunt of the accountability. At the executive level there is a lot of dependence on [us as executives] to make sure that [our] groups are delivering. If you start looking at the amount of expense dollars and the amount of revenue dollars that you have accountability for, you realize it's substantial. It's not to be taken lightly. . . . At the nonexecutive level, you don't really have as much accountability for things. . . . You may have touched some things but you weren't held responsible for it as much. At this level there are things that I may touch or have partial responsibility for . . . but I am going to be held more accountable for it. You are accountable for the result one way or the other.

Because of the "What have you done for me lately?" atmosphere that can exist at the executive level, you should consider what you can do to manage the stream of your team's results. Ensuring that results are delivered consistently and on time will enhance the reputation of your team and its ability to get things done in your organization. It is also important to communicate to key stakeholders and influencers in the organization the results your team achieves. Remember, the work doesn't speak for itself; you have to speak for the work.

## You Own the Results

There is an implicit message in the comments of Smith, Sannini, and Lanier: When you are an executive, the buck stops with you. The quickest way to damage your credibility with your team, your peers, and your boss is to pass blame on to someone else when a result that you're accountable for goes wrong or does not materialize.

In speaking about this dynamic, Lucien Alziari of Avon said, "The theme here is that you are not doing the work yourself, but the work that is being done ends up being yours because people will look at it and say, 'Well, that came out of so-and-so's team.'" Of course, when things go well, you share the credit with your team and let them know that you are sharing the credit. But, when the feedback you're getting is blame, you absorb it. When things go poorly, I encourage you to not wallow in the blame but to step up by acknowledging the problem and making a commitment to fix it.

Even if the problem resulted from the poor work of your team, don't broadcast that—it reflects more negatively on you than it does on them. After all, you are the one that either hired them or kept them on board. Your responsibility is to get the right people in the right roles, provide direction, and monitor progress. You are, therefore, accountable for their results. If those results are not up to expectations, your peers and boss won't care that it was your team's fault. They won't want a lot of excuses or explanations. They will just want you to fix the problem. If that means making changes in your team's roles and responsibilities or raising its level of talent, then do that. Learn the lessons that are there to be learned and act on them as you get back to the work.

## You and Your Peers Are Accountable for Solving Bigger Problems

Picking up accountability for many results is what distinguishes the executive leadership role from positions you've held earlier in your career. By the time you reach the executive level or are close to reaching it, you know from experience that getting results is usually not easy. The process requires problem-solving skills and the ability to adjust when things don't go as planned. As your career has progressed, you have undoubtedly refined your functional skills to the point where you frequently anticipate problems and make adjustments before they occur. As an executive, you will regularly be expected to develop solutions to problems that are outside your functional realm of expertise. The problems will be bigger and more complex. You will have accountability for addressing them in collaboration with your executive peers.

While you can draw on your functional expertise to solve problems, to deal with the more complex problems that executives face, you will have to add to your skill set. As Lucien Alziari noted earlier, "The skills that got you to the role are not the skills that are going to make you successful in the role."

Your functional skills are what Steve Smith of AEP calls "your ticket to the dance." Smith believes that he first reached the executive level because he had financial skills that people around him valued and respected, and that was his ticket to the dance. He adds, "Whether you are an excellent marketing person, an excellent lawyer, or an excellent operations person, there has to be some acceptance among your peers of a proficiency in one particular area." The perspective that comes from your functional proficiency is the foundation of how you add value as an executive, but, by itself, it is not enough. The extra value-added comes from how you take accountability for and participate with your peers in addressing issues that affect a broad range of results. Smith thinks that having broad-based problem-solving skills is one of the key accountabilities of an executive. He explains his point of view in this way:

> Usually when you are made an executive it is because you can fix problems. And very rarely are large, integrated companies problem-free. The reason you have executives is to manage those problems. I would say you are not going to be an executive without having to deal with some serious headaches. The reason you get promoted is because people believe you can alleviate those headaches.

Successful problem solving at the executive level requires deep collaboration with peers along with broad perspectives for looking at problems and opportunities. Chapters 8 through 10 address these requirements in detail.

## Setting Up Systems to Monitor Results

Learning to get comfortable with letting go of the details of execution is one of the bigger roadblocks to shifting from the responsibility mind-set to the accountability mind-set. Letting go of the details may require a couple of changes on your part. The first, as described in Chapter 5, is to get your ego out of the way by getting over the idea that no one else can do the work as well as you. The second is to set up one or more systems that enable you to monitor the responsibilities of your team and ensure that the results for which you are accountable are delivered in a way that exceeds expectations. Three of our executive mentors, Bob Johnson of Nextel, Bill Plamondon of Budget Rent-a-Car, and George Sterner of Raytheon, have complementary methods for staying on top of results while staying out of the details.

As senior vice president of national field operations for Nextel, Bob Johnson relies on regular on-site reviews to monitor the progress that his teams around the United States are making against the results called for in their business plans. Drawing on his decades of experience in the telecommunications industry, Johnson has come up with a process for conducting reviews that builds and sustains focus, momentum, and trust among the members of his extended team. Here is how he describes the process:

> I don't do all of the work that is in the business plan. However, I do follow up and make sure that the work gets done. That is one of the reasons I travel a lot. We have a regular schedule of operations reviews. The idea of those operations reviews is to

make sure that the team knows that their work is important and that we want to see the results, good or bad. [When I was coming up,] the scrutiny and detail [of operations reviews] could be brutal sometimes, but we don't do it that way. We do it in a matter-of-fact, metric-oriented way that is about holding teams accountable. . . .

[The basic approach is,] "I left you in Los Angeles six months ago and I gave you six months' worth of the business plan that we all agreed was appropriate. Now, I am going to come back and check to see how you did." And that is all it is. It should be expected as opposed to a punishment. In the cases when people are doing well, it is a great opportunity for the visible recognition because I am not going to be in L.A. tomorrow. I might not be back for three or four months, so I am going to tell you and your team, "Wow, good review. You guys are doing a great job."

It is a pretty rare occasion when you walk in and have a nasty surprise on a six-month review. If you have trust, you will have that awareness. Frankly, our metrics would surface things even if I didn't hear back from my team.

During his career in the car rental business, Bill Plamondon learned that one of the most effective ways for him to monitor results was to identify the right metrics and apply them at the appropriate level. He explained that, in the rental business, two key measurements focus on the number of cars rented and the speed of washing returned cars. The way those measurements are tracked depends on the responsibilities of the person doing the tracking. Plamondon describes it this way:

If you think about the rent-a-car business, the perspective of the person who is washing the cars or renting the cars is based on what they do within the next fifteen minutes to an hour. Their metrics are generally how many people did you handle in an hour? How many cars did you wash per hour? If you were to

look at the next level up, their supervisor, she is actually looking at what happens in the shift or in eight hours. And then if
you look at the next level up, somebody should be looking at
twenty-four hours and somebody else at the next level up after
that should be looking at thirty days. . . . If, as you move up in
the organization, you continue measuring what you were measuring, then there is no need for you because you are operating
from the old perspective.

Johnson and Plamondon each make some points that support the
habit of picking up accountability for many results. They both rely on
correctly determining the measurements that will allow them to
track results. Explicit in Plamondon's comments and implicit in
Johnson's is that review of those measurements has to be set at a
level that enables the executive to get the information needed to
track results without getting mired down in too many details. The
routine that Johnson has established with his operations reviews
gives him a regular look into the results and a recurring opportunity
to praise, coach, or correct his teams' performance. Conducting the
reviews on-site also gives Johnson an opportunity to build relationships with his team leaders and assess how they are interacting with
their teams.

George Sterner of Raytheon also emphasizes the importance of
setting up routines and systems that enable you to "sample the
strength of your staff." For Sterner, this process is about learning
whose judgment and performance he can trust implicitly and who
needs more ongoing attention. As he moved to different command
assignments in his Navy career, Sterner learned an important lesson:

The first day you get there, you probably believe most of your
people all the time. That's the last time you believe most of
them all the time. There are going to be strong ones and not-
so-strong ones. Building trust is a very personal thing . . .
understanding who you can trust and who is going to bring you
the right information and perspective is key. Information is

widely available but some of it is going to be worth a lot more because those that provide it really understand the issues and they are able to explain it. You quickly need to sort out where to put your energy with your staff.

## Accountability and Empowerment Go Together

Developing and shaping your staff so that they consistently meet the desired level of performance creates the opportunity for everyone to play at the next level up. For you, as an executive, having a staff that you can empower to deliver results enables you to take the broader perspective that is expected of you. For your staff, the empowerment that comes through your picking up the accountability mind-set and letting go of the responsibility mind-set leads to their professional development and job satisfaction. Let's turn back to Bob Johnson and his thoughts on how well-executed accountability and empowerment create successful executives and teams:

> One of my well-founded principles in leadership is adherence to both empowerment and accountability. As a leader, you probably got where you are because you were good at what you do. With increased responsibility, you can't continue to do everything yourself. So empowerment is very important because it is at the essence of your future success in a number of ways. One, because you have to let the people understand how they can be successful and how they can help you and the business be successful. Two, empowerment is an ongoing recruitment and retention tool. If people think that you will give them latitude, not only do they feel it and stay with you and become loyal to you, that word spreads. You want to work for this guy or woman because this is really a good place and a good environment.
>
> Where many developing leaders fall short is in not holding people accountable. It has to be very clear that if you are given the

latitude to deliver something to the business and ultimately the shareholders, you have to perform. There are consequences for not performing. I don't mean to say that in a threatening manner, but it has to be very obvious. [You want to be able to say,] "This is great. I love what I do. It is fabulous." The flip side is, "I missed my targets and there are some ramifications to that."

If a team understands the accountability approach they will hit the targets on their own. You don't have to continue to remind them how important that is. Those two things—empowerment and accountability—go hand in hand and form one of the core beliefs of my approach to leadership.

Picking up team reliance, defining what to do, and accepting accountability for many results are the transformative steps you can take as an executive to build the team presence required for next-level performance. Your advancement through the uncharted terrain of the next level continues by adding elements of organizational presence.

(10 **TIPS**)   **For Picking Up Accountability for Many Results and Letting Go of Responsibility for a Few Results**

1   To be accountable for many results, make sure you have a strong team and that you are clear in defining what to do.

2   Learn to derive satisfaction from the fact that the work got done, not that you did it.

3   Let go of taking personal responsibility for every outcome.

4   Shift your passion and energy from narrow functional interests to broader strategic interests.

5   Take a look at the questions you regularly ask. Doing so should provide some insight into whether you're operating in the tactical realm of responsibility or the strategic realm of accountability.

6   Support your team's efforts by strategically managing the timing and communication of their results.

7   Share the credit with your team when things go well; absorb the blame when they don't, act on the lessons, and move on.

8   Build new skills in working with your peers to solve the more complex problems that end up on executive plates.

9   Set up clear systems with regular time frames to monitor results.

10  Develop your team through empowerment and holding them accountable for their results.

# The Foundations of Organizational Presence

# PICK UP LOOKING LEFT AND RIGHT AS YOU LEAD

## LET GO OF LOOKING PRIMARILY UP AND DOWN AS YOU LEAD

Beginning with this chapter, we shift the focus from how successful executives lead their functional teams to how they demonstrate presence in the broader organization. If I had to support the concept of organizational presence with one piece of advice, it would be *broaden your field of vision.* That process begins with learning to focus your attention on your peers to the left and right while also paying attention to those above you and below you in the organization. It sounds simple to pay attention to what your peers are doing, so you may be surprised to know that failure to establish collaborative relationships with colleagues is one of the leading causes of executive derailment. In research conducted by the Corporate Leadership Council, failure to build partnerships with peers and subordinates was cited by 82 percent of survey respondents as one of the primary reasons executives fail in their jobs.

## Two Teams, Not One

In my career as an executive and a coach, I have seen a number of leaders fail because they could not overcome what I call "vertical tunnel vision." Everyone knows what tunnel vision is. I add the word *vertical* to the phrase because it helps describe the problem for new executives. If you are only looking vertically, up to what your boss wants and down to what your team is doing, you are missing at least half of the picture. As a new executive, you are now part of two teams. You are still a member of the functional team that you lead, but you are also part of the leadership team of your organization. Because of this dual membership, you have more relationships and agendas that need to be managed. Too often, because of vertical tunnel vision, new executives overlook the full range of the relationships they need to cultivate.

Mary Good of Blackboard has seen the impact of vertical tunnel vision over the course of her career. She says, "One of the things that I have seen happen over and over with people derailing is a lack of political astuteness around . . . building relationships with stakeholders. Somebody will manage up or they will manage down. They won't think about managing sideways. . . . It's easy to have a tendency not to do that when you are so focused on getting the work done and driving to meet what your boss or the board or somebody else says."

I made this mistake myself when I was recruited to Columbia Gas Transmission as VP of human resources. I knew that my boss, Cathy Abbott, wanted me to focus on changing the culture of the company from slow and stodgy to quick and nimble. I had first heard about Cathy a few months earlier when *BusinessWeek* ran a two-page story on her under the headline "Cathy Abbott is No Good Ol' Boy." Her nickname in the industry was "Hard-as-nails Abbott." When she hired me I *really* wanted to do a good job.

I thought the best way for me to get started was to travel in the field to get a feel for the company. Because our operations extended from the Gulf of Mexico to upstate New York, we had HR staff stationed along more than 16,000 miles of natural gas pipeline. A few weeks after arriving at Columbia, I started traveling out to the field to meet the staff and learn more about the business. This wasn't a bad thing to do in and of itself, but I overdid it. After three or four weeks of travel with only a few days at headquarters each week, I began to receive feedback that my executive peers were wondering where I was.

I had quickly developed an acute (and, fortunately, brief) case of vertical tunnel vision. I was looking up to what Cathy wanted and looking down to learn more about my functional team. By not giving time or attention to looking left and right, I caused myself to be disconnected from the concerns and agendas of my colleagues on the senior leadership team. For the leader of a function whose job was to support the rest of the organization, that was a mistake. To make matters worse, my executive colleagues had a lot of expectations about what they wanted from HR and by not being around enough I quickly found myself underwater with the workload.

Fortunately, Cathy was quick to correct my course. She called me one day and suggested we go get a beer together after work. As we were waiting on the elevator outside her office to leave, she looked at me with an "I know something about you" kind of look and asked, "So, this is a little steeper climb than you thought it was going to be?" "Gee, what was your first clue?" I replied. Over a couple of beers, Cathy gave me some very focused and helpful coaching about what was expected of me as a member of her executive team.

Learning how to shape and meet the expectations of two different teams is one of the most challenging aspects of entering the executive ranks. You will likely feel pulled, at first, between meeting the demands of your functional team and those of the executive team. This will be particularly true if you have been promoted from a lower-level functional leadership position. As you assume executive responsibilities, your functional team may not recognize or appreciate the additional demands on your time and attention. Moreover, they may have the expectation that your primary role with the executive team is to advocate their positions or initiatives. It is not. As an executive, your primary responsibility is to help shape, advocate, and enact the broader organizational agenda. You will do that in concert with your executive peers and with the support of your functional team and the support of the teams of your peers.

In this chapter, we'll take a look at what it takes to broaden your field of vision to the left and right while maintaining an appropriate degree of focus both upward and downward in the organization.

## Looking to the Left and Right

When you were an individual contributor or functional leader, you probably could get a lot of things accomplished on your own through focus, doggedness, and will. As an executive, you will no longer to be able to accomplish the things that matter most on your own. It may be counterintuitive, but it's true. The issues, and the relational politics around them, are more complex at the executive level. At the next level, interdependence replaces independence. To get things done, you have to know who to work with and who to talk to. You need to know what their interests are and how you can support them. You have to communicate your agenda clearly and act in a way that causes your peers to want to support it. As Donna Morea of CGI-AMS told me, "When you are on an executive team, it is influence only. There is no authority." When Donna shared this insight with me, I was reminded of one of my favorite professors in graduate school, the late Richard Neustadt. Professor Neustadt wrote the political science classic *Presidential Power*. One of the central tenets of Neustadt's book is that, regardless of all the resources available to the office, the power of a U.S. president lies in his ability to persuade. If persuasion is the currency of power for the president of the United States, I think that it probably is for corporate executives as well. My experience, and that of the executives I interviewed for this book, certainly suggests that is the case.

There are five important elements of getting things done by persuading and influencing those on your left and right:

- Get to know your peers

- Build trust

- Establish credibility

- Collaborate with your peers

- Show up as an equal

## Get to Know Your Peers

Most of the successful executives I know or have interviewed believe that one of the most important things to do as a new member of the executive team is to get to know your peers. Steve Smith of American Electric Power believes that it is critical to "understand what others are responsible for, what their scope is, and to learn about what it is they do every day and how what they do impacts you." Donna Morea agrees with this advice and offers this strategy for newcomers to the executive team:

> The one thing I would do if I were new to a team is meet with every single person on the team to understand who they are and where they are. What I would not do is come to the first meeting and start stabbing around about the issues without knowing much history or much about the dynamics of the team.

When coaching clients who are new to the executive team, I always encourage them to follow the approach that Morea recommends. I know from asking my clients' peers for feedback that approaching new colleagues with a sincere interest in who they are and what they do goes a long way toward establishing productive relationships. When preparing for introductory meetings with their new peers, I encourage my clients to ask open-ended questions such as these:

- What are the key outcomes that will make this year successful for you and your team?

- What kind of support would you like to see from me and my team to support your success?

- What is working well that my team should keep doing?

- What would you like to see my group start doing or stop doing to be more effective?

- If you were to look out twelve to twenty-four months and envision my group as completely successful, what would you see in terms of results and the mind-sets and behaviors that drive results?

- What advice or counsel do you have for me as a new member of the senior leadership team?

These kinds of questions have a number of benefits. First, they show that you have an interest in the agenda and perceptions of your colleagues. Second, open-ended questions show that you are open to feedback and doing what you can to support your colleagues. Third, they open up the conversation in a way that is likely to lead to your gaining some useful insights. Fourth, by approaching the conversation with sincerity and a willingness to listen and learn, you help build trust.

## Build Trust

I recently coached one of my clients in a financial services company to use Morea's approach with key colleagues who head different lines of business within the company. My client is a high-potential leader who is one of the top three or four industry experts in his specialty. The senior leadership of his company would like to see him apply his talents and knowledge on a broader stage. He is clearly capable of doing so, but to do that must let go of some of the sense of ownership he has around his specialty. He has, in fact, received feedback from senior colleagues that he is somewhat standoffish and not as collaborative as they would like him to be. In a coaching session, I encouraged him to schedule a meeting with the leadership of a key line of business to just ask questions similar to the ones in the preceding list. My client was a bit amazed and very pleased with what he learned in the conversation. "I always thought," he told me, "when they asked questions about how we were structuring a deal, that they didn't trust me or wanted to question my team's decisions. What I learned from talking with them is that they are basically fascinated by what we do and just want to learn more about it." From that conversation, my client also learned more about the goals of the line of business and new ways that he can use his expertise and that of his team to support them in achieving some key business results for the company. I know this process sounds simple. It is simple—but its potential to build trusting relationships is huge.

Open and regular communication is the catalyst for trust between peers. When communication is lacking, people tend to make assumptions and create stories about the actions and motives of others. This is especially true in a business environment in which executives are accountable for goals and objectives that often have very high stakes attached to them. To complicate matters further, these goals can sometimes seem to be in conflict with each other. Regular communications can smooth out the rough edges in relationships and build trust by minimizing the assumptions and rumors that come up when peers don't communicate with each other.

One executive I know addressed this problem by organizing a weekly fifteen- to twenty-minute update call with his executive peers. Those who are in the office meet together face to face; those who are on the road call in for the meeting. The agenda is informal. The meeting is basically an opportunity for the members of the group to check in with each other and talk about what's going on that week and what's coming up in the next week. The group has found that these weekly check-ins serve as a preventative to the misunderstandings and false assumptions that can bubble up when everyone is running hard to meet their goals and may not stop to bring others along. Their communications routine also helps build a sense of a shared agenda and allay the competitive dynamics that can occur between peers. If you're not already having regular check-in conversations with each other, it's worth thinking about how you and your peers could benefit from them.

## Establish Credibility

I first met Steve Smith when the two of us worked for Cathy Abbott on her executive team. As Abbott was building the executive team she needed to support and accomplish her agenda, she made a number of changes in the roster of the team. She tapped Smith, who had been in a new business ventures role, to take over the CFO position for the company. Steve's predecessor had developed a reputation as someone who used the budgeting process to play "gotcha" with the line-of-business heads. In his new job, Steve realized that he needed to make some changes in the process and approach to position himself as a collaborative member of the senior executive team. In doing so, Steve established his credibility as a peer and as someone interested in the success of his executive teammates. This is what he says about his thinking and actions in those first few months as CFO:

When I first came into Columbia, I was a VP of business development and I did a bunch of things and became known by some of the other senior folks. Then Cathy decided she needed a new CFO and named me to that position. It was apparent to me that the annual budgeting process was just a nightmare. The finance group did their own budget and the marketing group did their own budget and then we had a grassroots operating budget in there as well. It always came up that we needed $100 million more than we had. It was just awfully inefficient and it consumed a lot of energy for the entire organization. I stepped back and looked at it and I said, "God, this is so unproductive."

And so I said, "We are not doing this anymore." Everyone developed their own P&L or their own budget that they owned and input into the system. Our job in finance became to just aggregate, publish, and analyze the data. Then as a senior management team we could all look at it, analyze it, and figure out what levers we wanted to pull to make things happen.

When I went to that approach, it was kind of a risk. I wasn't sure if people would play ball because they hadn't been playing ball under the old system. It used to be that we would get into these big meetings with fifty people around this huge conference table and end up getting in arguments about what the numbers meant. It was totally unproductive. In making my change, I turned the ownership over to the businesspeople and just cut out an immense amount of work and frustration that they would normally have to go through every year to meet the old guidelines. Once that was cut out, people noticed it and then a month went by, two months went by and then they really noticed it. They would say, "My God, we did a tenth of the work and got three times as far."

So there was this huge emotional leverage that I think developed for me and my team because we freed up time, resources, energy, and hassle for a large number of people. Their lives got better and I got the benefit of that. They looked around and asked, "Well, who can I bestow all of my thanks on? Oh, it's this guy because he did it and now we're a lot better off and I feel better about that." So, in the space of six to nine months, I got a lot further than I ever would have if I had not done that.

As you move to the executive level, take stock of your opportunities to establish credibility with your peers quickly. If you are in a support function, your opportunity may be around making the lives of your colleagues easier or more productive. If you are leading a line of business, your opportunity may be around partnering with a colleague to win new business or reduce expenses. Or your opportunity to establish credibility may be to declare what you're going to accomplish and then deliver on that commitment in the time frame that you said you would.

## Collaborate with Your Peers

Collaboration works when the parties involved place equal emphasis on maximizing results and maximizing the power of relationships. Jay Marmer, a senior executive with Hydro Aluminum North America, has found in his career that collaboration is the best way to drive long-term sustainable results. Marmer talks about learning how to collaborate when he was an up-and-coming manager with General Electric:

> [What worked for me was] elevating my thinking process to a level where I got my point heard, but I was also being responsive to my colleague's point of view on the issue. It turned into more of a collaborative approach to solving problems as opposed to my way or acquiescing to the other person's way. That was a big learning for me along the way. . . . [Collaboration was about] forming a partnership where you are interdependent upon each other and working together for a shared result. It was beyond compromising. When you compromise, you get

something and they get something, and that's nice, but it really isn't the ultimate win-win. With collaboration, the ultimate reward is that you both get what you want.

The conditions for a collaborative approach are having high concern for achieving results while, at the same time, having a concern for building strong relationships. In taking a collaborative approach, it is critical to move past arguing positions and to take the time to uncover underlying interests. You can begin the collaborative process with a colleague by agreeing to ask each other open-ended questions and really listen to the answers. Here are some questions that I have found useful in building collaborative results:

- What are you trying to accomplish?

- What will that mean to you and the organization?

- What can I or my team do to help?

- Where do our interests overlap?

- What could we do to create mutual benefits where our interests don't overlap?

In his career at AOL, Pepsi, and other large companies, Mark Stavish found that the most effective executives "spend a lot more time working across other people's organizations. They are looking for opportunities to combine work, maximize relationships, and share information and ideas." Collaborative executives, Stavish says, "typically have great integration skills. They can get people across different organizations to work together. Interestingly, a lot of the time we call those operational skills. We say an executive is a great operating executive. It's just that they have the capacity of getting sales to work with manufacturing and manufacturing to work with customer support. When those folks talk about the things they really like, it's that integration of the work that really gets them going. I think those are the kind of executive skills that we ought to be selecting for."

When, earlier in his career, Stavish worked for a leading company in the hospitality industry, he regularly spent time coaching executives to a higher level of performance. Often, this coaching focused on helping his internal clients develop the skills and habits of collaboration. He found that what set the high-performing executives apart from their average peers was that they took the time to focus on the agendas of others rather than just focusing on their own. Stavish shared with me the story of one executive he coached and the straightforward plan they put in place to shift the perception of this person from a loner to a team player:

> I worked with a marketing guy who was one of those very talented guys with a ton of great ideas. His number one issue was that he didn't like to socialize his ideas with his colleagues because he, one, thought it was a waste of time and didn't want to waste other people's time and, two, as he said, "We should be able to just work these things out in the senior staff meeting."
>
> He was getting feedback that he was coming across as the Lone Ranger and surprising people with his initiatives. So I said to him, "You know what, socializing ideas is really important." I said, "You ought to spend more time, maybe 75 percent of your time, working outside of your organization and understanding what these regional VPs want and what they need," and he said "I don't get that." My reply was, "Your job isn't to do the best branding in the world. Your job is to figure out what they think is the best branding."
>
> So we created a little strategy for him where he would spend several days a month doing nothing but having customer sales meetings and then sharing his conclusions with the rest of the organization. He wasn't thrilled with that approach and felt like it was brownnosing his colleagues, but he was willing to give it a try. What he found was that, in addition to laying the politi-

cal foundation that he needed to implement his ideas, he had been missing some things and that, once he incorporated them, things worked much better.

Sometimes, the barrier to collaboration is not a reluctance to engage but a certainty that you already have the right answer and don't need any additional input. The point, frankly, is not so much having the right answer as it is getting the input and buy-in that creates support for the right answer. David Levy, president of the Corcoran Gallery of Art in Washington, D.C., and former president of the Parsons School of Design, has learned over time the importance of collaboration to getting things done. He says, "What I have learned over and over, and continue to learn, is that people want to be consulted. . . . No matter how much you believe you are right, you need to talk to other people. You need to hear other opinions."

## Show Up as Equal

There is a give-and-take quality to the art of collaboration. As a new executive, you want to be sure to not set up a dynamic that has you giving assistance far more than you're receiving assistance. The goal is to keep a roughly equal balance of credits and debits in your collaborative accounts with your peers. In the field of negotiation, there is a concept known as reciprocity. To establish reciprocity with a negotiating partner, you offer assistance or make a concession on one issue to gain the right to ask for assistance or a concession on another issue down the road. The same concept applies to collaboration between executives. After offering or responding to a request from a peer, do not be afraid to make a request in turn. The give and take of making and responding to requests helps build relationships and establishes mutual respect.

Jay Marmer told me that he received some good advice on this topic from a more senior executive at GE. As the newest member of his business unit's management team, he says,

[I found myself] working in an organization where I was really the junior guy on the team. There was one guy who was a former professor at Princeton. There was another guy who was running a big part of the business and he, too, was an extremely intelligent guy. These guys were overwhelming. I remember my boss telling me, "Whenever you get in a meeting with these guys, if they lay four or five things on you to do, you come back and give them one or two things that they have to do." I did that and it really formed a partnership where we were dependent upon each other and working together for something as opposed to them just dumping on me. It really highlighted for me the concept of collaborating and working together for a shared result.

To have the credibility to make requests, as Jay suggests, you have to do your homework. It is important to understand what is important to your peers and what you have to offer that helps them accomplish their agendas. Likewise, it is important that you understand what they have to offer that you can request in order to achieve your objectives. To show up as a credible peer, it is also important to have a clear and grounded point of view about what needs to be done to carry out the business strategy. Your point of view needs to encompass a clear understanding of what you and your team need to contribute to the strategy as well as what your peers need to contribute.

## Looking Up into the Organization

By emphasizing the need to look left and right, I am not suggesting that you ignore looking up to the most senior executives or down to your team and the teams of your peers. Obviously, there is a lot of information that you need to both give and receive along the vertical axis.

## What, Not How

One of the most important things to focus on with senior management is developing clarity about what success looks like to them. Chapter 6 explored picking up the habit of defining what to do and letting go of the habit of telling how to do it. Those same principles define how to approach your relationship with executive management. Spend time with them up front to ensure that you clearly understand their definition of what you need to do. Remember that, unless they say otherwise, you are not relying on them for their ideas on how to do it. From time to time, when I am conducting feedback interviews for a client, senior management complains to me that the client checks in too much for feedback on how he is performing or what he should do next. As one senior executive said to me once, "If I have to tell him how to do his job, why do I need him on the team? I hired him to be the expert and go get it done. I shouldn't have to tell him how."

It is critical, however, that you understand what success means to your senior executive and the top team. What are the metrics that need to be met or exceeded? What's the deadline for completion? Who has to be happy with the result? These are just some of the questions that need to be asked to define success. Make sure that you take the time to ask them. Also, ask your boss how often you should provide updates and what information should be in those updates. Defining the protocols around communication can help you strike the right balance between the overcommunication that can cause annoyance and the undercommunication that can lead to anxiety on the part of your boss.

## Solutions, Not Problems

Just about everyone who makes it to the executive level has learned the importance of bringing solutions and not just problems to the boss. This goes back to the comment from the senior executive who expressed frustration with being asked to constantly provide advice on how to do the work. Most of my executive-level clients and the high-potentials who are moving to the executive level don't have a problem with the practice of bringing solutions and not just problems to their boss.

The exception to this rule is that I occasionally see situations in which the senior executive needs to step in to resolve conflicts among direct reports. Needless to say, this is not an activity that senior executives enjoy or look on with favor. As David Levy, president of the Corcoran Gallery, says,

> First of all, I expect my team to see themselves as a team. I want to see that they are willing to work with each other and support each other even when that may be a little bit counter-intuitive. I expect them to look for ways in which their institutional relationships can come together and be mutually reinforcing.

Unless you're working in a completely pathological organization, your boss expects you and your peers to work as a team. Use the advice provided by the mentors in this chapter to establish the strong peer relationships that will enable you as a team to provide solutions and not problems to your boss.

## Looking Down into the Organization

In the context of looking left and right to build peer relationships, there are a couple of points to make about managing your relationships with the people in your organization who are below the executive level.

### Stay Connected

In *Primal Leadership: Realizing the Power of Emotional Intelligence,* Daniel Goleman, Richard Boyatzis, and Annie McKee describe a malady that, in spite of its name, can afflict executives at any level. They define *CEO disease* as the "information vacuum around a leader created when people withhold important (and usually unpleasant) information" (p. 93). Most executives will tell you that they don't like unpleasant surprises. When CEO disease takes hold, unpleasant surprises are almost guaranteed. The quickest way to develop a case of the disease is to send signals that you are not open to or won't listen to valuable feedback about what is going on in the organization. When you take on an executive level title, you are much less likely to get the real scoop on what's going on down into the organization solely because, unless they are shown otherwise, people have a natural tendency to distrust anyone with an executive title after their name.

This lesson was brought home to me personally several years ago when I was a vice president at Columbia. As you may have guessed, I am an avid reader and sometimes will buy multiple copies of books that I really like and give them away to others. One of these books is *Slowing Down to the Speed of Life* by Richard Carlson and Joseph Bailey. When I was at Columbia, I gave away a couple of cases of this book with many of the copies going to folks in my HR department. The response to the book was so positive that I offered to set up a weekly discussion group for anyone interested in talking about it over the course of several weeks. One of the participants in the group was an administrative assistant named Lisa. Before the group began meeting, I interacted with Lisa with some frequency but not for any great lengths of time. A couple of weeks into the discussion group, Lisa sent me an e-mail thanking me for the group and the book and to say that she was getting a lot out of both. That was nice to read, but the punch line for me was when she concluded by saying that the group had been a particularly good experience for her because she had gotten to know me better and had been dissuaded from her previous view that all vice presidents and above had "green blood and horns!" That was a real wake-up call for me. It let me know how much more I needed to do to allow people to know and trust me as a person and not just as a member of the executive team.

Martin Carter of Hydro Aluminum North America has found in his career that he needs to build a network that extends throughout the company to stay grounded about his leadership and informed about what is really going on. He describes it this way:

> I do rely heavily on the network in the organization to give me feedback on how I am perceived. . . as well as the real issues underlying the business. [By doing this,] I get a tremendous amount of information. I don't, and shouldn't, react to all of it, but I do rely on others to ensure that I get a better and more realistic picture of the business. If I just relied, at least initially, on what I get from the formal line, my picture would be some-what distorted. It takes a while, though, to break down those formal barriers.

In his naval career, retired admiral George Sterner developed what he called a "network of eyes" that kept him tuned in to what needed his attention. Sterner's goal, he says, was to encourage at all levels of his organization the idea of "bring me bad news, but don't surprise me. Get it to me early enough that we can do something about it." Throughout his command career, Sterner made it a point to stay visible and to interact with his sailors in their environments. He did not want them to feel like it was a big deal to talk with the admiral. With this tone of approachability, Sterner found that his net-work watched out for him and gave him the early warning he was looking for on things that needed to be adjusted or redirected. In my experience as a coach, I regularly work with executive clients who need to increase their level of approachability. The skills they need to adopt typically include some of the characteristics that Sterner exhibited to his organizations:

- Staying visible and available

- Listening without interrupting or appearing distracted

- Asking open-ended, nonthreatening, questions

- Showing a sincere interest in people

## Stay Grounded About Your Own Team

In spite of your best efforts, your team will not always perform perfectly. When they don't, it's important to show openness to feedback about their performance and act on it appropriately. Most of the time, this will mean taking the feedback back to your team and helping them learn from their mistakes. Sometimes, it may mean that you need to take more dramatic action. When presented with negative feedback from a peer on your team's performance, respond by asking open-ended questions to learn more about what happened as well as the perceptions of what happened. Make your best effort to engage the peer providing the feedback in a conversation that fosters learning rather than complaining or competition.

The flip side of this issue is striking the right balance on praising your team. Certainly, you want to let senior management and your peers know what your team has accomplished. Remember, the work doesn't speak for itself; you have to speak for the work. At the same time, though, pay attention to when enough is enough. Joni Reich, senior vice president, administration, for Sallie Mae, has seen a number of executives damage their credibility by overselling their teams in a highly competitive way. She says,

> I have seen executives at a very high level completely derail themselves because they were so caught up in the idea that their team is the best team and their team deserves all the credit and that that other team is no good. That type of petty bickering and preschool behavior is amazing to me at this level, but sometimes it happens—and it's the surest way for someone to derail.

Finally, help your team stay grounded by helping them understand where they and their work fit into the bigger picture. Clearly, they should understand how they need to contribute and what is required of them. They may also need your leadership to understand that their agenda is not the only agenda in the organization. Just as you, as an executive, need to look left and right to succeed, you can help your team members play at the next level by encouraging them to look left and right as well.

**10 TIPS** **For Picking Up Looking Left and Right as You Lead and Letting Go of Looking Primarily Up and Down as You Lead**

1   Avoid vertical tunnel vision by paying attention to your peers on your left and your right.

2   As an executive, make your primary concern the broader organizational agenda, not advocacy for your team's agenda.

3   Remember that, at the executive level, success depends more on interdependence than independence.

4   Get to know your executive peers by asking them open-ended questions that demonstrate your interest and willingness to help.

5   Build trust with your peers by conducting regular group meetings to share information and touch base.

6   To collaborate with your peers, move past arguing over positions by taking the time to understand each other's underlying interests.

7   Work to establish a roughly equal balance of credits and debits in your collaborative accounts with your peers.

8   Look to your boss for a clear definition of what to do, not an explanation of how to do it.

9   To avoid unpleasant surprises, work on staying connected at all levels of the organization.

10  Raise your team to the next level by insisting that they look left and right to their peers in other functions.

# PICK UP AN OUTSIDE-IN VIEW OF THE ENTIRE ORGANIZATION

## LET GO OF AN INSIDE-OUT VIEW OF YOUR FUNCTION

Moving from one level to the next requires an increasingly broad perspective with each move up. As a functional manager, you tend to focus on what's helping and hurting in terms of reaching your particular objectives. In a sense, it really is all about you or at least you and your function. There is an old joke about the narcissist who, after going on and on about himself, finally says to his companion, "Well enough about me, what do you think about me?" When you're a functional leader, it's kind of like that. It's all about you and your team. When you look outside your team, it is probably to determine what somebody else can do to help you or to make sure that somebody doesn't get in your way as you try to accomplish your goals.

As you reach the executive level, the focus shifts from "me and my team" to "us as the leadership team" of the entire organization.

That shift from *me* to *us* needs to be quickly followed by an additional shift in perspective from *us* to *them*. The "them" in this case refers to all the stakeholders and competitors in the external environment. In this chapter, we'll talk about how to make those shifts. We'll start with the reasons that executives need to leave behind a function-centric approach to their work. This can be referred to as overcoming the "me mind-set." Then, we'll take a look at how to operate with an organization-wide perspective. This is about moving to the "us mind-set." Finally, we'll talk about how the best executives view their organization with an outsider's perspective to understand the context of the broader environment. This deals with the last shift of moving to a "them mind-set."

## Overcoming the "Me Mind-Set"

When you stop and think about it, it's really not surprising that many new executives have to deal with the challenge of overcoming the "me mind-set." The behaviors that get a lot of people to the executive level deal with a singular focus on accomplishing assigned objectives. As Steve Smith of American Electric Power says, "You have to be incredibly focused to move up that chain. . . . You are self-absorbed in what you do every day. That's a good thing at the lower levels because you are very focused on execution and getting stuff done."

To echo a theme from earlier chapters, what got you to the executive level is not what is going to keep you there. In our conversation about moving up, Smith went on to define the nature of the required change in mind-set: "As you move to VP, you still have to be concerned about where you fit in and how your group is viewed, but you also have to take a broader view of the organization and what your value is to the organization."

As you move to the executive level, the expectation is that you will shift your allegiance from what is best for you and your function to what is best for the leadership team and the organization. As a high-potential leader below the executive level, you were likely encouraged and rewarded for going out and getting it done within the narrower band of your responsibilities. Organizations need leaders who can take a piece of the overall plan and make it happen. That singularity of purpose is a luxury that successful executive leaders realize they can't afford. At the executive level, there will be times when you will need to modify your functional agenda or even put it aside for the overall good of the organization. Laura Olle, senior vice president of Capital One, explains how many senior executives view the change that new executives need to make:

> My expectation of the new vice president is that they will do the right things for the company even if it means individually they might not meet their objective or whatever is on their particular agenda. You have to be much, much more self-sacrificing as a VP. In this company, directors run groups. They run projects. They are very focused on delivering results around that project or that team or that group. . . . I think it's a huge leap to move from focusing on what's best for your own results to focusing on what's best for the results of the entire company. I don't believe that the behavior that gets you to vice president is the behavior that you are expected to continue.

What are the function-centric behaviors that get you there but need to stop at the executive level? Let's answer that question by focusing on what you need to start doing to develop an outside-in view of the entire organization.

## Get Out of Your Silo

If your modus operandi has been to accumulate or even hoard resources to ensure the success of your function, you will need to quit doing that to be a successful executive. Too often, new arrivals to the executive team are slow to recognize the walls they build around themselves by hoarding resources. Steve Smith describes the issue this way:

> I think one of the biggest mistakes that new VPs make is that they can be too myopic. They focus on building a power base in terms of size or budget dollars without really seeing how the value proposition for them and their team applies to the rest of the organization. They are focused inwardly (instead of out-wardly), so they create a silo within a large organization and their focus is on perpetuating that silo.

As we discussed in Chapter 8, power and influence at the executive level come from collaboration and sharing information and resources with your peers. Steve Smith described this kind of approach as the type that leads to a result of $2 + 2 = 5$. That's the kind of synergy you want to shoot for as you shift from a "me mind-set" to an "us mind-set."

## Replace the Small Picture with the Big Picture

If you're in silo mode, it's difficult to see what really matters to the big-picture success of the organization. In her career, Joni Reich of Sallie Mae has seen new executives fail by overlooking or ignoring the bigger picture. In our conversation for this book, she cited a number of small-picture behaviors that executives should avoid:

- Overadvocating for your group

- Discouraging your team from cooperating with other teams

- Skirting team responsibility for mistakes or problems

- Not pitching in to solve big-picture problems

- Fighting over key personnel

In my case, I can think of a number of colleagues or clients whose success depended on changing one or more of these behaviors. As Joni Reich says, "This type of small-minded thinking is a way for someone to demonstrate that they are not a big-picture person."

## Be Willing to Take One for the Team

As noted earlier, you have to be more self-sacrificing at the executive level. Sometimes this will mean that you have to "take one for the team" by turning over some of your resources or key people for the good of the larger organizational agenda. Laura Olle of Capital One expects every vice president to make sacrifices. For example, she says, "If your star performer, who you rely on the most, is needed someplace else in the company, for the greater good of the company, you have to let that person go." Obviously, you cannot consistently give up every key resource you have or you will end up being completely ineffective. It is important, however, to strike the balance between what is best for your agenda and what is best for the organization's agenda.

## Connect Your Part with Their Parts

One executive described his role to me as feeling like the conductor of an orchestra. That metaphor is apt in thinking about becoming a successful member of an executive team. As you've progressed through your career, you've likely become so adept with a particular "instrument" that you've now been asked to take first or second chair in the orchestra. Just because you're great with the cello, doesn't mean that the orchestra doesn't need woodwinds or percussion. Your conductor (your CEO) expects you to know how to play with the rest of the group. Marc Effron of Hewitt Associates sees this as a developmental opportunity for a lot of his clients. He describes it this way:

These are people who have been extraordinarily strong individual contributors for most of their lives. It is what has allowed
them to get to the point where they are today, but often they
then have to broaden their skill sets. It doesn't matter how
smart they are or how effectively they can do a deal, they truly
need to understand how other parts of the business fit with
their part. The question is, How can they help expand the overall pie and not just their slice of it? That is a real challenge for
people because it is a fundamentally different skill set. I think
most people have found that the most difficult transition is to
go from "Here is what I am good at" to "Here is how we manage the business together."

## Take a Look Around

In Chapter 8, I said that if I were to boil down all of the advice about
how to operate as a member of the executive team to one idea, it
would be to broaden your field of vision. This is a particularly important idea when your path to the executive level has included a lot of
time in nonexecutive roles in the same function in the same company. As Steve Smith said earlier, this type of career path can sometimes lead to myopia. Cathy Abbott, former CEO of Columbia Gas
Transmission, has seen the same dynamic at play with a number of
new executives. She says,

> If you are promoted from within—particularly if you have been
> in the corporation for a long time and understand the organiza-
> tion—it's important to remember that you do understand it, but
> only from one seat. The real work is to understand what it takes
> for the whole executive team to accomplish what they need and
> what part you will play in accomplishing that. The idea that you
> may need to give up resources or priorities in order for the
> whole to succeed is a really counterintuitive thing for many
> people.

Based on Abbott's comments and the perspective of our other executive mentors, you can no doubt see why looking left and right as you lead is so important to overcoming the "me mind-set." Moving into the "us mind-set" requires the broader field of vision that comes from consistently taking a look around to see what others are doing, what they need, and how you can help. Taking a look around also helps you better identify the people who can help you and how they can do it.

## Moving into the "Us Mind-Set"

Lucien Alziari of Avon summed up what moving into the "us mind-set" is about by saying that the shift executives need to make is "business first, function second." In talking further about this, Alziari said, "The transition that people need to make is to think about the business as a whole and then reverse engineer into what that means for your function to support the business. It isn't about getting the best functional agenda. It's about getting the right agenda to support the business as a whole." Implicit in these comments is the idea that to make the contributions that are expected of you as an executive, you have to view yourself as a leader of the business and not just your function. We'll talk more about how to make that shift in Chapter 10, on the importance of picking up a big-footprint view of your role. In the current context of picking up an outside-in view of the organization and letting go of an inside-out view of your function, the focus needs to be on appreciating the nature of the contribution you're supposed to make.

### Think Bigger

The simplest way to describe how you should think about what is expected of you is to just say, "Think bigger." Remember, it's not just about you and your to-do list anymore. It's bigger than that, and your peers and bosses expect you to demonstrate that you understand. Your perspective and field of vision must expand. Bill Christopher of McKesson Process Technologies (MPT) provides a good example of the nature of the change that has to occur. He is a relatively new vice president, having recently moved up from a slot as director in charge of a key client relationship for MPT. He told me that, in his role as a director, "My focus was the customer that I had. They were huge, with about 50 percent of the revenues for the business unit. That was important, of course, and that was my sole focus, not how the business unit was going to do." When he became part of the executive team for MPT, Christopher recognized that he had to broaden his focus. As a vice president, he is expected to think about and act on behalf of the business as a whole. He describes the shift in this way:

> Now the role I am in is even beyond just what the business unit can do. It's about what McKesson is going to do overall. What is our contribution to that? Basically, any time I am making any decision about spending or strategic direction, I try to think about what it is going to do to McKesson overall.

As Christopher's focus has expanded, his knowledge and business literacy have had to grow along with it. To be effective as a member of the business team requires the kind of intellectual curiosity that he demonstrates when thinking about how his decisions affect McKesson as a whole. To fully anticipate and appreciate the impact of his decisions, he needs to be increasingly familiar with the key financial indicators for McKesson and the factors that most affect those indicators. He needs to understand the priorities of the overall corporation and how his decisions interact with and affect those priorities. This is the kind of outside-in thinking and behavior for which executives, as leaders of the entire organization, are responsible.

## Bring Your Team Along

As you begin to put the business first and your function second, you will need to help your functional team understand your operating context. Practicing perspective transference can play a key role in boosting their understanding. Cathy Abbott says, "Part of your job is to take what the whole organization is trying to do and bring that back to your team and help them understand what they need to do in order for the whole to succeed." By transferring your executive-level perspective to your team, you will help ensure that the right work is done for the right reasons. You will also be accelerating the development of your team by giving them the information they need to play a level up.

There are many different ways to bring your team along by practicing perspective transference. Based on some of the earlier chapters of this book, you have probably picked up on the fact that I am a big fan of the open-ended question. I believe that asking your team leaders questions such as "How do you think our priorities match up with the priorities for the company as a whole?" or "Given where the company is headed, what do you think we need to do next?" is a great way to start a conversation that leads to learning and appropriate action on their part. Another resource available to you as an executive leader is to appropriately share your insight on the process and rationale behind high-level decisions.

As an executive coach, I am always pleased to hear the direct reports of my clients tell me, "My boss shares information and perspective with us that my peers in other functions don't get." The impact of that kind of sharing is huge in the way it raises the effectiveness, morale, and development of the functional leadership team. Given how effective it is, I am surprised that I don't hear about it more often. Of course, as an executive you will be privy to information that cannot go any further than the communication between executive principals. As Sue Stephenson of the Ritz Carlton Hotel Company points out, "If you've got a good solid relationship with your team there is always the desire, if you are a strong communicator, to share as much information as you can. So you try to balance what is appropriate to share and what isn't appropriate to share. As you move into more senior roles there is far more confidential information that would be risky to the business if you were to breach the confidentiality agreement that you make as a group. That can be difficult." In my experience, I have found that it is helpful to state up front for your team that you will share as much information as you can with them, but there will be times when it is in everyone's best interest for certain information not to be shared.

## Thinking About "Them"

Sometimes executive teams can become so focused on "us" that they don't think enough about "them." Business history and management strategy books are full of examples of executive teams that became so enamored with their way of doing things that they ultimately failed their company by not understanding or believing what was going on out there. This phenomenon is sometimes known as "drinking your own bathwater"—or, by the more technical term, "smoking your own dope." All kidding aside, the failure to regularly look at the organization from the outside in is a fairly common mistake that executive teams make. As a new member of the executive team, you may well have the opportunity, as a fresh voice, to encourage your colleagues to challenge their assumptions and take a broader look around. Even if you find that your peers are not particularly receptive to this, you owe it to yourself, your team, and your business to regularly think about "them." Mark Stavish, formerly of AOL, thinks that where executives often fail is that "they don't challenge their own organization enough. They don't ask if the assumptions are right. Is our direction right? Are we doing things the way we really should be doing them? There is no active questioning."

To get a sense of how much the environments we operate in can change, you need only look at the list of the thirty companies that made up the Dow Jones Industrial Average (DJIA) in 1976 and compare it to the list of Dow components in the spring of 2005. Only eight of the companies on the Dow in 1976 were still there in 2005. Some of the companies that dropped off the list include American Can, AT&T, Bethlehem Steel, Chrysler, Eastman Kodak, International Paper, Sears, Union Carbide, and Westinghouse. Who's to say that some of today's giants—Citigroup, Hewlett-Packard, Home Depot, Intel, Microsoft, Pfizer, Verizon—will still be on the Dow thirty years from now? If there is one thing that the history of this average shows, it is that the business environment is constantly changing. Only one company, General Electric, has been a continuous member of the DJIA since it was created in 1896. It's interesting to note that when Jack Welch took over GE in 1980, he demanded a large-scale questioning of the assumptions that had led to GE's success. In spite of the demigod status that Welch developed over the years, Jeff Immelt, who succeeded Welch in 2001, has established himself as a leader by questioning the assumptions that led to success in the Welch era. There has been so much said and written about leadership at GE that it is tempting to write at least some of it off as hype. When you look at the hundred-year-plus track record of the company, however, it certainly looks as though the innovation that comes from questioning assumptions and looking at the outside world works for them.

Jay Marmer of Hydro Aluminum experienced this early in his career when, as a young manager for GE, he heard Jack Welch speak at a leadership conference in Connecticut for high-potential leaders in the company. He says,

> This was back in the eighties and the war between Iraq and Iran was going on. Welch was talking about activities in the

Middle East and the military build-up there and different things related to the environment in that part of the world. I remember sitting there thinking, "My God, we're here talking about how to make a refrigerator and this guy is off on what's happening in the Middle East." The point is that there are so many things you have to be mindful of as a leader in the business. I realized I had to get much more broad-based in my thinking.

Cathy Abbott was known as an innovator and broad-based thinker in the energy industry. She told me that, for executives, "a big piece of your job is to shift to scanning the market conditions to look externally at the corporation and ask what ideas are out there that need to be brought to your organization and that require a different set of skills." When I worked for Abbot, all of us on the executive team were expected to scan not just the energy industry but any industry for new ideas that we could bring back to create a higher level of performance at Columbia. This is the kind of approach that fuels growth and innovation. It is what leads to the changes needed to adapt to new competitive pressures and opportunities.

When you are an executive, it is particularly important to get out of your day-to-day environment once in a while. Mark Stavish shared a memorable idea with me: "A leader ought to be looking for the paradox." In making a case for regularly challenging your assumptions, he adds,

[As an executive, you] should actively be questioning everything you do. Not throughout the organization because you will drive everybody out of their minds, but you should be actively questioning if you have the right strategy in place. The only way you do that is to get out of your office and go talk to customers and people outside of the organization. Figure out what your competitors are doing.

Cathy Abbott echoes this advice, encouraging new executives to do more external networking: "There is a much greater external orientation that you have to have if you are going to be successful. You need a greater outside-in orientation, and you have to be much more attuned to the external market."

Picking up the outside-in view of the entire organization and letting go of an inside-out view of your function is one more step in advancing through the uncharted terrain of the next level. Like so much of the rest of the process of personal development it takes to become an effective executive leader, it can feel strange and uncomfortable to make this shift. As you move from "me" to "us" to "them," you will find that your comfort level rises as you see the results that come from broadening your field of vision.

(10 **TIPS**) **For Picking Up an Outside-In View of the Entire Organization and Letting Go of an Inside-Out View of Your Function**

1   As you reach the executive level, remember that the expectation is business first, function second.

2   Build your influence through collaborating, not through accumulating or hoarding information or resources.

3   Recognize when you may have to contribute key people or resources for the good of the whole.

4   Focus on expanding the size of the pie and not on getting the biggest slice for yourself.

5   Identify what the executive team needs to accomplish together and how you can contribute to that.

6   Think bigger by asking yourself how your goals affect the goals of the entire organization.

7   Work on increasing your understanding of the key financial indicators and strategies for the whole business.

8   Practice perspective transference with your team so that they too can play at the next level up.

9   Tune in to the external environment by regularly questioning your assumptions and operating practices.

10   Expand your perspective through external networking.

# PICK UP A BIG-FOOTPRINT VIEW OF YOUR ROLE

## LET GO OF A SMALL-FOOTPRINT VIEW OF YOUR ROLE

Expectations change when an executive title appears after your name. Your boss, your subordinates, your peers, all the other employees in your organization, your customers, and people you haven't even met yet will all develop stories about you. Everyone will have different expectations about what you should be doing and how you should be acting as an executive. They will project their expectations onto you, and most of the time you won't even know it because they won't tell you they're doing that. Honestly, many of them won't even be aware that their expectations of you have changed. In many ways, it's less about their expectations of you than it is their expectations of someone with your title. You can like it or not like it—but, either way, when you have an executive title, expectations are not only different—they're higher. You are now a designated leader in your organization. In most organizations, leaders are expected to deliver the goods.

If you are promoted to the executive level on a Monday, you may feel like the same person you were last Friday. That's good. Hold on to the idea that who you are is no different just because you're an executive. That will help you stay grounded. However, get used to the idea that what others now expect of you is different. Some expectations will be reasonable and some won't. Some won't even be rational. You are now dealing in the twin realms of logic and emotion. There are certain things that executive leaders are logically expected to do; but stakeholders can project a lot of emotional baggage onto executives. Hope and fear, loyalty and betrayal, excitement and despair—I know it sounds like a soap opera, but these are just some examples of the emotional dynamics executives have to address. One of the most dangerous things you can do as a new executive is fail to recognize the full range of expectations that are being projected onto you.

Learning to deal with these new expectations is the focus of this chapter. Even though you are still the same person you were before you became an executive, you have to pick up a big-footprint view of your role. Conversely, you have to let go of the idea that you can operate off the radar screen and be effective as an executive. You have to let go of a small-footprint view of your role. The big-footprint role that you'll have as an executive will present itself in two major ways. First, you are going to be much more visible to all the stakeholders in your organization than you used to be. Second, because of your increased visibility, you will be expected to make a bigger impact in the organization. We'll talk about how to handle both of those issues in this chapter.

## Living with a Higher Profile

Let me start with a few quick stories that illustrate what it's like to live with the higher profile that comes with being an executive. The first of these stories comes not from business but from show business. One of my best friends from third grade on is a fellow named Michael Cerveris, who has built a successful career as an actor and musician over the past twenty-five years. (I'm proud to say that Michael won a Tony award in 2004 for his role as John Wilkes Booth in the Steven Sondheim musical *The Assassins*.) One of Michael's first big breaks came in the late 1980s when he was cast as British rocker Ian Ware in the television series, *Fame*. Michael and I were both living in New York City at the time and along with my wife, Diane, got together one afternoon to go to the movies. I remember little of the movie, but what happened afterward was very memorable. Diane, Michael, and I were walking down the sidewalk outside the theater when three or four teenage girls passed us in the other direction. A few seconds after they were past us, they turned and screamed in unison, "Ian! Ian!" Michael was kind of embarrassed but told us that that had been happening a fair amount since he was cast on *Fame*. We talked about how strange it is, as a celebrity, to have people know who you are without your knowing who they are.

Several years later, I experienced a little bit of the same phenomenon when I joined Columbia Gas Transmission as vice president for human resources. (I know, it's not as glamorous as playing a rock star on TV, but how many executive jobs are?) Because of the publicity surrounding Columbia in the local community and because of the numerous changes in the management team that my new boss, Cathy Abbott, had made, there was a fair amount of buzz surrounding me when I came to the company. I remember feeling surprised to find my picture on a placard in the headquarters lobby my second day on the job. A group that was leading a reengineering initiative had designated me as an executive "change champion" and put my picture up along with the other executive champions. It didn't really matter what they knew about me (most of them hadn't even met me yet); since I was the VP of HR, I was a change champion. It was as simple as that. As I walked the halls of headquarters those first few weeks, I was a bit taken aback by all of the people who addressed me by name when I didn't even recognize them, let alone know their names. Suddenly, I was on the radar screen and it was uncomfortable and disconcerting. I didn't have teenage girls screaming my name (however cool I might have thought that to be earlier in my life), but I understood a little bit how Michael must have felt that day in New York. It was weird.

A number of the executives I interviewed have experienced the same feeling. Laura Olle began her corporate career at Marriott and then moved on to Freddie Mac before joining Capital One. She told me that one of her biggest surprises in reaching the executive level was the degree to which people were and watching and "reading into" what she was doing. The depth of attention that people paid to what she said and did was noticeably greater for her as an executive than it was earlier in her career, even though she'd had some important jobs in large companies. Sid Fuchs of Northrop Grumman has experienced the same thing—but probably to an even greater degree because he is president of a significant business unit within the company. He has noticed that, as he has taken on larger executive roles, one of the biggest changes for him has been the amount of attention he draws. "I'm onstage," he says. "I'm in a fishbowl."

Let's talk in some depth about the implications and opportunities that accrue with being in the executive fishbowl. Your footprint as an executive can have a greater impact for good or for bad. As you consider the opportunities that go with having a bigger footprint, it may be helpful to remember a maxim from the U.S. Army that retired general Steve Rippe shared with me: "The further up the flagpole you go, the more your ass shows." Particularly when dealing with subordinates in the organization, new executives can use the following tangible strategies to ensure that they stay modestly covered as they ascend.

## Act Like an Ambassador

When you become an executive, you become what Nextel SVP Bob Johnson calls an "ambassador of the culture." It doesn't matter what your responsibilities are or how deflated or inflated your executive title is, you represent the top leadership of the company. If you think about what makes a good ambassador, it is not so much that they are diplomatic as it is that they think before they speak. They anticipate the possible effects of their words and adjust what they say for the desired effect. You have to do the same thing as an executive. Your words will have a greater impact because of your higher role. Remember that the way you use your words can dramatically affect the morale of the organization.

## Check Your Sense of Humor

A sure way to damage morale and sink productivity is to casually speak about emotion-laden issues such as downsizing, reorganization, compensation and benefits, and performance goals. I've learned this lesson the hard way, as have many other executives. It's often necessary for new executives to rein in the sarcasm or irony in their sense of humor. One executive I interviewed told me he realized this early in his executive career when a reorganization was being planned and, knowing that it would result in responsibility shifts but not job losses, off-handedly said to a group of employees that he would let them know after the reorganization whether they still had jobs. This executive was fortunate to have a feedback loop that let him know he had scared everyone to death and he needed to go back and explain that he was joking.

Needless to say, if you're on the receiving end of a joke about job security, it's not really funny. It's surprising to me how many executives miss the point that people lower in the organizational structure know executives have the power to eliminate jobs. Therefore, jokes about job security, no matter how lighthearted or innocent they may be, just aren't funny. The antidote for this problem is for executives to put themselves in the shoes of the people listening before they speak. Ask yourself, "If the positions were reversed, how would I respond to or what would I think about this comment?"

## Think Before You Speak

Another bad habit some executives have is "just thinking out loud" in mixed company. A couple of years ago, I spent time around a corporate department in which a senior vice president would regularly muse aloud in front of anyone on various options for restructuring the department to respond to new business conditions. Most of his scenarios involved reductions in headcount. As you can imagine, the rumor mill and the fear factor in the department would go into overdrive every time he did this. Just about the time things would start to settle down, he would have another "just thinking out loud" conversation with a couple of new people and the process would start all over again. This department spent a year in needless turmoil. It never did restructure. For some reason (lack of empathetic perspective and an ego on overdrive would be two of my guesses), this executive could not process the damage he was doing as a senior vice president who thought out loud indiscriminately about what might happen. The result in this case was employees who were perpetually distracted from the real work that needed to be done.

In other situations, I've seen executives who have been shocked to see their subordinates act on casual musings they've made in meetings. I recently talked with a friend who is a high-potential leader in a Fortune 500 technology company. He told me that, a few years ago, the company CEO, in speaking at an internal leadership conference, mentioned that he would like to see his company recruit some talent from firms like "Company X." Six months later, my friend's company was full of new managers from "Company X." There had been no official directive to go out and recruit those managers other than the CEO's comment at the leadership conference. But, a large group of motivated executives and high-potential leaders heard their CEO say that it would be nice to have some people like those at "Company X;" so they immediately acted to fulfill his wish. This wasn't necessarily a bad thing for my friend's company, but the influx of so many managers from one source has clearly had some unanticipated and unintended consequences on its culture and business execution. When you're an executive, it makes sense to pay attention to the old saying, "Be careful what you wish for" (especially out loud).

## Leave Air in the Conversation

Another dynamic to watch out for is sucking all the air out of a conversation by pushing your point of view too hard. When you are debating with peers, it may be more acceptable to press your point. When you are having a conversation with subordinates and want to generate an open discussion on options, be careful not to dominate the conversation. While you may think you are just having a spirited conversation, your subordinates will likely read it as you imposing your will as an executive.

I recently worked with a new executive client who throughout his career has demonstrated a passion for debating the technical merits of different potential solutions. This tendency served him and his employer well when he was an individual contributor because it led to better outcomes. Once he became an executive, that same approach tended to shut down solutions because subordinates did not want to risk their position by debating a vice president. The irony was that my client enjoyed the debates and welcomed them—he just failed to recognize at first that the outcomes were more one-sided now that he was a vice president. Fortunately, I was able to share feedback from his subordinates that helped make him more aware of the need to back off a bit in deference to his bigger footprint in the organization.

## Invite Feedback

One way to demonstrate that you are open to feedback is to invite it. As a member of your organization's executive team, you have both the opportunity and the obligation to seek out feedback from employees about their concerns and what is on their mind. In my years as an energy industry executive, I found that informal visits and conversations in the field were among the most useful and rewarding things that I did. Because the historic culture of Columbia had been one of command and control, the employees were not used to executives coming out to ask what was going on and what was on people's minds.

In my first year of traveling to pipeline compressor stations and district offices from Louisiana to New York, I often had people tell me that I was the first human resources VP they had ever met. As my executive colleagues and I traveled the pipeline in those first couple of years, it took the employees some time and experience to decide they could trust us. One of the ways we achieved that was to ask questions and really listen to the answers. It was also important for us to show that we were willing to answer hard questions ourselves. As Columbia was making changes in the way it did business, there was certainly more than one time when I stood at the front of the room and listened while employees aired their complaints about what they thought were the stupid things we were doing as a management team. While it wasn't always fun to let people blow off steam, doing so enabled us as a leadership team to demonstrate that we were taking a new approach to the way people were expected to contribute to the company. In a company where the traditional way of doing things was for supervisors to tell employees, "Dig the ditch from here to here and then come back and I'll tell you what to do next," the executive team's willingness to listen sent the signal that we wanted everyone to engage their brains and not just their backs.

In talking about the importance of executives' using their footprint to send a positive message, Nextel's Bob Johnson described how he and his peers act as ambassadors of the culture:

> We have 3,500 people here in Reston, Virginia, but there are 19,000 people at Nextel all over the country in around 160 locations. We have business units set up everywhere. The visibility aspect is absolutely critical because while we might do webcasts with the president and COO or other types of mass communications with their name on an e-mail distribution, a lot of times you are the most senior person that employees see on a regular basis. That reinforcement of just being there and being a willing recipient of feedback is key. It is important to take feedback when you are making visits to the field locations. The employees don't want me to defend why it is what it is. They don't want me to do anything but to encourage the feedback and really just take it in and listen. Even if you don't do anything about it, at least they feel like you listened. The ideal situation is if you hear it and do something about it.

Getting out and talking and mixing with employees on a regular basis is probably the most effective way to shape the business culture you and the rest of the executive team are trying to create.

## Living with Other High-Profile Types

If you've spent any time watching the Discovery Channel, you have no doubt seen films of animals in the wild fighting each other for territorial supremacy. It could be a couple of rams butting horns until they're dizzy or a couple of hippos battling it out for control of a muddy pond. As your executive footprint gets bigger, your days may sometimes feel like tryouts for the next season of *Wild Kingdom*. This is when the path through uncharted terrain can become uncomfortably bumpy.

## Choose Your Path

At the executive level, battles for control can be common. As someone operating at that level, you have a choice to make. One path is approaching the battle for control as a zero-sum game with clear winners and losers. If that's the direction you choose, I don't have a lot of advice for you other than to prepare yourself for a career full of stress, mistrust, and not really accomplishing much of long-term consequence. Clearly, all you have to do is read the business press to recognize that plenty of executives do choose this path. Most of them, I think the record shows, eventually end up losing. (Think Enron, Health South, WorldCom, Tyco, AIG, and Sunbeam, for a start). Buddhists call it karma; the Bible refers to it as reaping what you sow. I usually think of it as what goes around, comes around: How you treat people is, in the long run, how you will be treated.

The other path you can choose begins with picking up the habit of looking left and right as you lead. Getting to know your peers, building trust, establishing credibility, and seeking to collaborate with your teammates are the building blocks of learning to live successfully with other high-profile types. You may find that your collaborative approach is sometimes not reciprocated. Even if that's the case, I encourage you to stay true to the path you've chosen. Don't be a pushover, but, when you take a tough or aggressive stance, make sure that you're choosing a strategic response to the situation rather than reacting with unchecked emotion. By doing this, you'll feel better about yourself and get more done in the long run.

## Choose Effectiveness over Being Right

One of the most common barriers that new executives have to overcome in working successfully with peers whose footprints are equally big is the "I'm right" syndrome. Almost by definition, your peers at the executive level are going to be experts in something. All of you probably got to the executive level by being right again and again. It's what brought you to the dance. You've got to let it go. Marc Effron, the leader of Hewitt Associates' study of the top twenty companies for developing leaders, explains why:

> I think one of the challenges in transitioning from the individual contributor role is recognizing it doesn't always matter if you are right. You may very well be right, but people are going to get sick of hearing you fight for your idea because you are right. . . . The right solution is the one that actually solves the problem with all members of the group being relatively happy that they are moving in that direction. Part of the right solution is recognizing that consensus in most organizations will be more important than individual brilliance.

> That is very difficult because a lot of these folks have been successful because they have been right for a long time. They have analyzed the stock right, they have come up with the right chemical compound, they have done whatever it is in their technical area that they needed to do to demonstrate that they are really, really good. At the end of the day, though, standing on principle or excessive argument around why you are right gets you absolutely nowhere.

Closely related to the "I'm right" syndrome is what I call "smartest kid in class" disorder. Sometime between grade school and college you probably came across the kid who always had the right answer and was only too happy to let the teacher and everyone else know about it. The other kids usually don't like the smartest kid in the class. The same is true with executive teams. If you insist on your answer always being the one best right answer, you can easily end up being seen as aggressive and overly critical. You can end up being branded as someone who is difficult and doesn't get the big picture. When everyone at your level is operating with a big footprint, and the ego issues that come with that, you are much more likely to be successful by directing some effort to making your peers feel smart and successful. All of you probably are smart or you wouldn't be executives. Don't waste time on proving how smart you are to your peers. Spend your energy on bringing the group together to come up with smart outcomes.

# Mind Your Message

Before Roger Ailes became the force behind Fox News, he was a very successful political consultant and television news producer. About twenty years ago, he wrote an interesting book with a great title: *You Are the Message*. The idea behind Ailes' title is important. The bigger footprint you have as an executive means that the messages you send will be broadcast to a wider audience. Many of those messages will be to internal audiences, but quite a few will be to people and institutions outside your organization. Once again, your executive title identifies you as an ambassador of your organization and its culture. To the degree that your company is known in the external community, it will be judged in part by how you handle yourself. You are the message for yourself and for your company. Assume that there are always people out there forming impressions based on the message you send. Let me share my experience and that of other executives about what to do and what *not* to do.

## Represent the Organization

The importance of minding your message was brought home to me early in my career. Following a stint on Wall Street, my next move was to return to my home state of West Virginia to be director of research and strategic planning for the governor's economic development office. One morning, I was scheduled to deliver a speech to a small group at an economic development seminar sponsored by one of the state universities. That same morning, the *Wall Street Journal* ran a front-page article criticizing West Virginia. The article contained dozens of factual errors and, I thought, was a gratuitous cheap shot. I began my speech by referencing the article and sharing my anger and thoughts about it. I then went on to my prepared remarks. The next morning brought a sense of panic when I looked at the front page of the local newspaper and saw that an official from the governor's economic development office (me!) had criticized the *Wall Street Journal* in a speech the day before. Apparently, some reporters had been in the room at the seminar and hadn't bothered to identify themselves. Of course, I hadn't bothered to ask who they were. If you've been in politics, you have probably learned that it is not a great idea to speak on behalf of your boss unless you have been cleared to do so. I had not and was quickly running through the scenarios of what my next job was going to be after the governor fired me for speaking out of turn. Fortunately, my boss and his boss, the governor, were understanding and I got off with a valuable lesson learned. From that point on, I realized that when you are carrying a title from an organization, you represent that organization.

This dynamic can play out in the press and, in the age of blogs, can play out immediately. Therefore, it's important to always present yourself, and your company, in a way that you would be willing to read about on the front page of the *Wall Street Journal.* In my interviews, I asked several executives to talk about how much care they take to protect their image and that of their company when they're in the public eye. Concern about image runs the gamut from when they're at the mall with their family on the weekend to when they're hosting a party for customers during an industry convention. The questions they ask themselves range from "What message do I want to send?" to "What impression do I want to leave?" I'm not suggesting that they are trying to send a message that is inconsistent with who they really are. They are being intentional about putting out a message consistent with how they and their company are at their best.

## Look the Part

One aspect of message management that I think is often overlooked today is appearance and dress. My observation is that the era of "casual Fridays" is either coming to an end or at least being redefined upward. Even in companies where formal business attire is not expected, the standards for appearance, especially for the leaders, are rising. When I am conducting feedback for clients on what they can do to be more effective leaders, I sometimes hear comments like "Tell him to stop dressing like he's still in college."

A good rule of thumb for how to dress as an executive or high-potential leader is to look at the successful people one level up and follow their lead. If they're wearing jackets and tailored slacks or skirts, consider going in that direction yourself. It is also important to pay attention to how your client base dresses and to show respect by dressing to that level. I know of one senior executive in a company that works a lot with high-level government officials. This executive is fond of flannel shirts and corduroy jackets with patches on the elbows while his government clients go with conservative suits and dress shirts. From what his peers have told me, this executive, who is brilliant, has lost credibility with his clients because of how he dresses. You can argue that appearance shouldn't matter, and you might be right. I like to remind clients that it's important to remember the difference between what should be and what is. The truth is that appearances matter to most people whether they recognize it consciously or not. A sales executive recently told me that he has started requiring his team to wear formal business dress when meeting with clients because it's the equivalent of "putting on the pads and the helmet in the NFL." When you are an executive, you almost always acquire a new image expectation along with your bigger footprint. It makes sense to understand that expectation and live up to it. Doing so will eliminate needless distractions from the message you are trying to deliver.

## Hang Up and Drive

Let's talk about another source of message distraction that executives need to eliminate: electronic devices that take your attention away from the people who are in the room with you. When you're in a meeting, put away the BlackBerry, cell phone, pager, laptop, Palm Pilot, and anything else that allows you to multitask. Remember, as an executive, you are onstage. People watch you for signals of who and what you care about and how much you care. Giving colleagues, at any level, less than your full presence and attention is a sign of disrespect and inattention. My clients who have stopped checking e-mail or doing spreadsheets in meetings have started looking and acting like executives rather than individual contributors on a caffeine buzz. Constantly playing with your cell phone in a meeting can be as damaging to your career health as talking on one while you're driving can be to your physical health. "Hang Up and Drive" is as good a bumper sticker for the office as it is for the car. Remember, with the big footprint of an executive, you are the message. Act accordingly.

## Play a Bigger Game

Bigger stakes and bigger expectations come with the bigger footprint of the executive role. One advantage of a bigger footprint is the political capital that comes with it. Political capital, however, is like physical fitness: If you don't use it, you lose it. As an executive, you are expected to take action and work with your peers to make an impact for the organization. To be more specific, you are expected to deliver a series of positive results over time.

Be prepared for the pace to move even faster than it did when you were a leader on the way to the executive level. Catherine Meloy, president of Goodwill of Greater Washington, spent most of her career as a senior vice president with communications and broadcasting giant Clear Channel. For new executives, she says,

> The part that changes is the immediacy of action which is expected. You know, if the top leaders think about it today, it needs to be done this afternoon. And that is the part that I think people who are getting into this, especially in the profit-and-loss business of a large corporation, need to know. There is always that funny thing about, What did you do for me today? It is almost, What did you do for me this minute? It's not that the approach is rude. It is just a very fast-paced world.

Executives get paid to make things happen and to solve problems. It requires resilience and creativity to do that. Paul McDermott of Freddie Mac makes the point that a big part of executive life is bouncing back from problems or moving around them to find solutions. McDermott says,

> That's what got you there. If you claim to be this person who has all of this energy and enthusiasm, you know, apply it. . . . The toughest thing to do when you're in an environment where it doesn't all automatically fit is to not feel sorry for yourself and recognize that there is still a lot to learn. Then you can figure out opportunities and, if you don't like something, you can help change it. I don't want to be one of these guys who walks in and says, "I've got a problem." I need to be able to say, "I've got a problem and here are three options that I think could solve it. Here is my recommended option and why."

As an executive, you will almost certainly find yourself in situations full of ambiguity and inertia. Don't just sit and wait to see what happens next. Figure out what would make a positive difference and work with your peers to make it happen. That is what will differentiate you from other executives who may be waiting to be told exactly what to do. The more senior executives probably won't tell you what to do. They expect you to figure it out and act.

If you're perceived by your peers and bosses as someone who uses their footprint to get things done, then you will build the political capital that will allow you to get more things done. It is important for your personal success and the success of your organization  not only to be someone who gets things done but to partner with others who get things done. As a director at Verizon, Mike Lanier has entered the executive ranks of his company. In our interview, Lanier described a dynamic that is true not just at Verizon; it's true in any organization with a broad-based leadership team:

> At the director level, you can tell that people are a lot more cognizant of who is performing and who isn't and who is going places. It is interesting that if you are perceived as going places, I think you get a lot more support from your peers. There is an awareness of who has that senior-level support because situations change so frequently. Any one of us could at some point be working for the other one and I think that may be part of the motivation for some people. I think there is also this situation where if a peer who has a lot of influence with senior management is pushing for something and you don't support it, they are likely to find a way to make it happen without your support, making you look like the nonplayer.

These observations paint a picture of what it looks like when executives are working well together. Sometimes you are in the lead role; sometimes you are in a support role. Either way, to use an Arab saying, the dogs bark, but the caravan rolls on. Things will continue to happen whether you're on board or not. If your goal is to make the most of the bigger footprint that is available to you as an executive, then you need to to be on board.

**10 TIPS**    **For Picking Up a Big-Footprint View of Your Role and Letting Go of a Small-Footprint View of Your Role**

1    Remember that your executive title will automatically raise your profile and the impact of everything you say and do.

2    Power imbalances can change the dynamics of humor. Consider your subordinates' perspective before making a joke.

3    Avoid the unintended consequences that stem from "thinking out loud" in front of subordinates.

4    Encourage feedback from subordinates by backing off a bit from a forceful presentation of your point.

5    Be an ambassador of the company culture by being visible and accessible to employees. Be sure to listen while you're being visible.

6    Keep your emotions in check by responding to, rather than reacting to, input or actions you don't agree with.

7    Be willing to choose an effective outcome with your peers over the desire to demonstrate that you're right on a particular point.

8    Because you are a representative of your organization to the public, give some thought to the message you send through your actions and appearance.

9    Build up capacity to get things done by using the political capital that accrues to you because you're an executive.

10    Be a part of the group that works together to get things done while others are waiting for direction.

# AFTERWORD

## LIVING AT THE NEXT LEVEL

If success at the next level comes down to just one thing, it may be the art of strategic choice. A common theme in the interviews I conducted for this book and in the lives of the successful clients I have coached is the importance of having the insight to pick up what you need and the courage to let go of what served you well in the past. Making the choice to pick up a new behavior or belief or to let go of one that is no longer serving you requires the capacity to step back and ask yourself, "Given what I'm trying to do or accomplish, is this serving me?"

Einstein is said to have defined insanity as doing things the way you've always done them and expecting different results. In the whirlwind of change, it is often difficult to step back to assess what is still working and what needs to change. The people who are most successful in dealing with change or navigating the uncharted terrain of the next level are those who choose to step back and get some strategic perspective on what is working and what isn't. They then apply that perspective, not just to their career, but to their life as a whole.

This book offers some fairly specific insights and advice about what executives need to pick up and let go of to successfully navigate the next level of their career. I encourage you, however, not to let the specifics obscure the bigger picture. The skill of strategic choice—of deciding what to pick up and what to let go of—has applications that extend far beyond executive life. Navigating uncharted terrain and making choices with incomplete information is no longer the exception but the rule in most aspects of life. Each of us has the opportunity to move forward through learning by doing, observing the outcomes, and making adjustments to our behaviors when necessary.

In the uncertain moments of navigating new experiences, confidence comes from relying on the core characteristics that serve you well in any situation. The courage to assess, make choices, and move forward comes from understanding how you are when you are operating at your best. In Chapter 3, I introduced a tool called the Life GPS, which can help you identify the characteristics that describe how you are when you're at your best, reinforce those characteristics through regular routines, and align your core characteristics in support of the outcomes that are most important to you. If you have not taken the time to create your Life GPS, I encourage you to re-read Chapter 3 and write one for yourself.

The Life GPS is based on the idea that each of us is a unique individual with a set of experiences, skills, and characteristics whose potential extends far beyond any one job or any challenge we happen to be facing at a particular time. At your best, you are bigger than the challenge facing you. You have advanced through uncharted terrain before and lived to tell the tale. You will do so again.

You are who you are and you have the daily opportunity to bring the best of who you are to everything you do.

I'm not a huge Woody Allen fan, but one scene from the movie *Annie Hall* has always stayed with me. As his relationship with Annie begins to hit the rocks, Allen looks into the camera and says, "A relationship, I think, is like a shark. You know? It has to constantly move forward or it dies. And I think what we got on our hands is a dead shark." Life is like that, isn't it? Isn't it about moving forward—advancing—taking that next step?

A verse in the book of Psalms says, "Your word is a lamp to my feet and a light to my path." The promise in that verse is that we are given enough information, knowledge, or wisdom to take the next step. While it might be nice or make us feel more comfortable to have a set of high-beam halogen headlights that illuminate the next two miles of road, all we are given is a lamp that lights the next few steps on the path. If you look back on your life, there are probably more times than not when it was enough to have a lamp. Advancing into uncharted terrain is about taking the next step and the next and the next after that. It's about developing consciousness around what is and isn't serving you as you take those steps. It's about retaining what is working, staying open to picking up new skills and mind-sets, and having the courage to let go of the behaviors and beliefs that brought you this far when they no longer serve you on your journey.

None of us can see everything that is ahead of us down the road. What we all do have is the opportunity to operate from how we are when we're at our best and to draw on those characteristics to create the outcomes that matter most. That's what moving to the next level, no matter what the terrain may be, is all about.

# APPENDIX A

## CREATE YOUR EXECUTIVE SUCCESS PLAN™ (ESP™)

Soliciting and acting on colleague feedback is a proven way to improve your performance as an executive. As you move to the next level, consider using this process for creating an Executive Success Plan (ESP) to maximize the value of colleague feedback. While it is possible to manage this process on your own, many executives find it useful to engage the services of an experienced coach. In addition to facilitating the mechanics of the process, an experienced executive coach can offer objective guidance and perspective that can enhance the development process. For information on how to select an executive coach, visit www.nextlevelexec.com.

## BUILDING EXECUTIVE PRESENCE

| Pick Up | Let Go Of |
|---|---|
| **PERSONAL PRESENCE** | |
| Confidence in your presence | Doubt in how you contribute |
| Regular renewal of your energy and perspective | Running flat out until you crash |
| Custom-fit communications | One-size-fits-all communications |
| **TEAM PRESENCE** | |
| Team reliance | Self-reliance |
| Defining what to do | Telling how to do it |
| Accountability for many results | Responsibility for a few results |
| **ORGANIZATIONAL PRESENCE** | |
| Looking left and right as you lead | Looking primarily up and down as you lead |
| An outside-in view of the entire organization | An inside-out view of your function |
| A big-footprint view of your role | A small-footprint view of your role |

## 1. Select a feedback team.

- Identify ten to twelve trusted colleagues from whom you would like some feedback. The group should be a mix of subordinates, peers, and people at higher levels of the organization. Your boss should be in the group.

## 2.  Ask for feedback.

- Share the Next Level model with each of your colleagues in a one-on-one meeting. Ask them which two or three elements of the model are most important to your success as an executive.

- Within the context of your two or three most important elements of the model, ask your colleagues to assess the things you do when you are at your best that you should keep doing. Take notes on their responses, which will provide ideas on the strengths you can leverage as an executive.

- Again, within the context of your two or three most important elements of the model, ask them to assess the things that you could start or stop doing to help you be and act more consistently at your best. Take notes on their responses, which will provide ideas on the steps you can take to be a more effective executive.

## 3.  Analyze the feedback.

- Analyze the notes from your feedback conversations. Make a master list of the primary themes regarding your strengths and what you could start or stop doing to be more effective.

## 4.  Select your high-leverage opportunities.

- Look for opportunities to apply your key strengths with new audiences or in new ways.

- Identify one or two things that you could start or stop doing to be more effective that, if well addressed, would have the biggest positive ripple effect on your success as an executive.

## 5.  Share and validate your conclusions.

- Share your conclusions with the members of your feedback team. Validate your conclusions with them on strengths and development opportunities. Ask for their specific thoughts on ways to leverage your key strengths. Also ask them for their one or two best ideas on specific ways you could improve in your high-leverage development opportunities. For example, if listening better is one of your development opportunities, ask for their ideas on how you could demonstrate better listening skills. Take notes on their ideas for how you could build on your strengths and improve on your opportunities.

### 6. Choose your action items.

- Review your notes and choose one or two items from the leveraging strengths ideas and one or two items from the development opportunities ideas that you are willing to consistently do over the next ninety days.

### 7. Engage your feedback team.

- Let the members of your feedback team know what you are working on and ask them for ongoing input on how you're doing on your action items. Tell them you would like to hear from them when they see things going well and when your performance could be better.

- Each week, make it a point to ask two or three members of your feedback team for a four- or five-minute update on how you're doing on at least one of your action items. Asking for a few minutes of feedback just after a meeting is one way to do this.

### 8. Check your overall progress.

- At the end of ninety days, ask each member of your feedback team for their assessment of your progress on your action items. Do they see a positive change, no change, or a negative change? If you have been diligent in following this process, they are almost certain to see a positive change. Ask them if they have additional ideas to further leverage your strengths

and opportunities. If they don't, ask them if there is anything else that they would encourage you to focus on in your
development.

### 9. Review and choose your next steps.

- Compare the summary feedback with your original data and
  decide what else you might focus on over the next ninety days.
  If there is something else, repeat steps 4 through 8 of the ESP™
  process. If there seems to be nothing additional to focus on,
  keep doing what you've been doing—including regularly asking your colleagues for feedback on how things are going and
  what you could do to be more effective. If your organization
  doesn't provide it, plan to ask for in-depth colleague feedback
  at least annually to ensure that you are still on track.

# APPENDIX B

## SITUATION SOLUTIONS GUIDE

There are numerous situations, such as entering a new company and leading a disruptive change, that occur with predictable regularity in most executives' careers. The following table identifies some of the more common situations executives find themselves in and matches them with some of the solutions discussed in *The Next Level.* For more in-depth analysis, follow the chapter reference for each solution.

## SITUATION SOLUTIONS GUIDE

| Situation | Solution | Chapter |
|---|---|---|
| First-time executive | 1. Take a learning stance to better understand the issues at the executive level and how you can make a contribution. | 2 |
| | 2. Act as a peer consistent with the cultural norms of your organization and executive team. | 2 |
| | 3. Prepare yourself to share points of view that add quality to the executive conversation and decision-making process. | 2 |
| | 4. Choose to take the time to establish and practice the routines that bring out the best in you. | 3 |
| | 5. Establish a process of regular communication with your boss that enables easy and effective information exchange. | 4 |
| | 6. Create opportunities to speak for the good work of your team and position your boss to share that information with his or her peers and boss. | 4 |
| | 7. Slow down enough to listen to the concerns and priorities of senior executives before rushing in with your opinion or plan of action. | 4 |
| | 8. To recalibrate the best way for you to add value, regularly ask yourself, "What is it that, given the perspective and resources I have as an executive, only I can do?" | 5 |
| | 9. Get very clear on the big-picture results that are expected of you and your team. | 6 |
| | 10. As you reach the executive level, remember that the expectation is business first, function second. | 9 |

| Situation | Solution | Chapter |
|---|---|---|
| Dealing with promotion to a more senior executive position | 1. Be prepared to act without having all the information you might like to have. | 2 |
| | 2. Break the cycle of continuous exertion by building into your calendar some regular time for recovery. | 3 |
| | 3. Leave space in your schedule to deal with the unexpected crises that will inevitably demand your attention and clear thinking. | 3 |
| | 4. Keep your perspective by remembering that you are not your job. | 3 |
| | 5. Be intentional about your communications' impact in the broader organization; frame your spoken and unspoken messages to create an environment in which people feel safe to share information. | 4 |
| | 6. Slow down enough to listen to the concerns and priorities of senior executives before rushing in with your opinion or plan of action. | 4 |
| | 7. Package your key issues and initiatives in crisp sound bites that outline their importance and the actions required for success. | 4 |
| | 8. Remember that presence begets presence. People will take more cues from your body language and tone of voice than they will from your content. | 4 |
| | 9. Train your ego to derive satisfaction from what your team accomplishes, not from what you accomplish. | 5 |
| | 10. Set up clear systems with regular time frames to monitor results. | 7 |

| SITUATION SOLUTIONS GUIDE continued | | |
|---|---|---|
| **Situation** | **Solution** | **Chapter** |
| Entering a new company | 1. Take a learning stance to better understand the issues at the executive level and how you can make a contribution. | 2 |
| | 2. Act as a peer consistent with the cultural norms of your organization and executive team. | 2 |
| | 3. Prepare yourself to share points of view that add quality to the executive conversation and decision-making process. | 2 |
| | 4. Develop a routine of visualizing the desired outcome and how you need to show up to get it. | 2 |
| | 5. Break the cycle of continuous exertion by building into your calendar some regular time for recovery. | 3 |
| | 6. Take time to regain your leadership perspective by "getting up on the balcony" to look at the whole picture of what's going on down on the "dance floor." | 3 |
| | 7. Be intentional about your communications' impact in the broader organization; frame your spoken and unspoken messages to create an environment in which people feel safe to share information. | 4 |
| | 8. Establish a process of regular communication with your boss that enables easy and effective information exchange. | 4 |
| | 9. Do your homework before important presentations by learning what is most important to the audience and the methods of communication that work best for them. | 4 |
| | 10. Don't wait to build a team that gets results. With a mediocre team, the pace at the next level will be too fast for you to keep up. | 5 |

| Situation | Solution | Chapter |
|---|---|---|
| Entering a new company | 11. In assessing your team, honestly ask yourself if you have the right people. If the answer is no, make changes quickly but with respect and compassion. | 5 |
| | 12. Get to know your executive peers by asking them open-ended questions that demonstrate your interest and willingness to help. | 8 |
| | 13. Look to your boss for a clear definition of what to do, not an explanation of how to do it. | 8 |
| | 14. To avoid unpleasant surprises, work on staying connected at all levels of the organization. | 8 |
| | 15. Build your influence through collaboration, not by accumulating or hoarding information or resources. | 9 |
| | 16. Identify what the executive team needs to accomplish together and how you can contribute to that goal. | 9 |
| | 17. Think bigger by asking yourself how your goals affect the goals of the entire organization. | 9 |
| | 18. Work on increasing your understanding of the key financial indicators and strategies for the whole business. | 9 |
| | 19. Be an ambassador of the company culture by making it a point to be visible and accessible to employees. Be sure to listen while you're being visible. | 10 |
| | 20. Be a part of the group that works together to get things done when others are waiting for direction. | 10 |

## SITUATION SOLUTIONS GUIDE continued

| Situation | Solution | Chapter |
|---|---|---|
| Feeling overwhelmed | 1. Get comfortable with changing what you do by letting go of the need to feel like a functional expert. | 1 |
| | 2. Be prepared to act without having all the information you might like to have. | 1 |
| | 3. Reframe your definition of what your daily contribution to the result should be. It should be about influencing others to create the result, not creating the result yourself. | 1 |
| | 4. Identify the interference that keeps you from performing at your best and minimize it. | 1 |
| | 5. Develop a routine of visualizing the desired outcome and how you need to show up to get it. | 1 |
| | 6. Break the cycle of continuous exertion by building into your calendar some regular time for recovery. | 2 |
| | 7. Take time to regain your leadership perspective by "getting up on the balcony" to look at the whole picture of what's going on down on the "dance floor." | 2 |
| | 8. Leave space in your schedule to deal with the unexpected crises that will inevitably demand your attention and clear thinking. | 2 |
| | 9. Keep your perspective by remembering that you are not your job. | 2 |
| | 10. Remember that presence begets presence. People will take more cues from your body language and tone of voice than they will from your content. | 4 |

| Situation | Solution | Chapter |
|---|---|---|
| Feeling overwhelmed | 11. In assessing your team, honestly ask yourself if you have the right people. If the answer is no, make changes quickly but with respect and compassion. | 5 |
| | 12. To recalibrate the best way for you to add value, regularly ask yourself, "What is it that, given the perspective and resources I have as an executive, only I can do?" | 5 |
| | 13. Remember, as an executive, you are a keeper of the what, not a master of the how. | 6 |
| | 14. When you are tempted to get involved in the how, ask yourself, "By spending my time on this activity or process, do I produce a significantly better result?" | 6 |
| | 15. Implement some simple levers of control that enable you to influence the quality of the results without doing the work yourself. | 6 |
| | 16. Learn to derive satisfaction from the fact that the work got done, not that you did it. | 7 |
| | 17. Let go of taking personal responsibility for every outcome. | 7 |
| | 18. Shift your passion and energy from narrow functional interests to broader strategic interests | 7 |
| | 19. Take a look at the questions you regularly ask. That should provide some insight into whether you're operating in the strategic realm of accountability or the tactical realm of responsibility. | 7 |
| | 20. Remember that, at the executive level, success depends more on interdependence than independence. | 8 |

| SITUATION SOLUTIONS GUIDE continued | | |
|---|---|---|
| **Situation** | **Solution** | **Chapter** |
| Leading disruptive change | 1. Take a learning stance to better understand the issues at the executive level and how you can make a contribution. | 2 |
| | 2. Be prepared to act without having all the information you might like to have. | 2 |
| | 3. Prepare yourself to share points of view that add quality to the executive conversation and decision-making process. | 2 |
| | 4. Develop a routine of visualizing the desired outcome and how you need to show up to get it. | 2 |
| | 5. Take time to regain your leadership perspective by "getting up on the balcony" to look at the whole picture of what's going on down on the "dance floor." | 3 |
| | 6. Leave space in your schedule to deal with the unexpected crises that will inevitably demand your attention and clear thinking. | 3 |
| | 7. Take into account where your audience is and where you want them to be in terms of thought, feeling, and action. | 4 |
| | 8. Be intentional about your communications' impact in the broader organization; frame your spoken and unspoken messages to help people feel safe to share information. | 4 |
| | 9. Package your key issues and initiatives in crisp sound bites that outline their importance and the actions required for success. | 4 |
| | 10. Increase your value added by positioning or interpreting the work of your team through the lens of your executive-level perspective. | 5 |
| | 11. In working with your team, focus on defining the desired outcome and making sure it is well understood. | 5 |
| | 12. Get very clear on the big-picture results that are expected of you and your team. | 6 |

| Situation | Solution | Chapter |
|-----------|----------|---------|
| Leading disruptive change | 13. Take time to stop and regularly recalibrate your perspective on what needs to be accomplished and the progress being made. | 6 |
| | 14. Build trust with your peers by conducting regular group meetings to share information and touch base. | 8 |
| | 15. To avoid unpleasant surprises, work on staying connected at all levels of the organization. | 8 |
| | 16. Think bigger by asking yourself how your goals affect the goals of the entire organization. | 9 |
| | 17. Practice perspective transference with your team so they can play at the next level up. | 9 |
| | 18. Tune into the external environment by regularly questioning your assumptions and operating practices. | 9 |
| | 19. Expand your perspective through external networking. | 9 |
| | 20. Remember that your executive title will automatically raise your profile and the impact of everything you say and do. | 10 |
| | 21. Power imbalances can change the dynamics of humor. Take your employees' perspective before making a joke. | 10 |
| | 22. Avoid the unintended consequences that stem from executives "thinking out loud." | 10 |
| | 23. Encourage feedback from employees by backing off a bit from a forceful presentation of your point. | 10 |
| | 24. Be an ambassador of the company culture by making it a point to be visible and accessible to employees. Be sure to listen while you're being visible. | 10 |
| | 25. Build up your political capital to get things done by using the capital that accrues to you because you're an executive. | 10 |

## SITUATION SOLUTIONS GUIDE continued

| Situation | Solution | Chapter |
|---|---|---|
| Having trouble with executive peers | 1. Remember that, at the executive level, success depends more on interdependence than independence. | 8 |
| | 2. Get to know your executive peers by asking them open-ended questions that demonstrate your interest and willingness to help. | 8 |
| | 3. Build trust with your peers by conducting regular group meetings to share information and touch base. | 8 |
| | 4. To collaborate with your peers, move past arguing over positions by taking the time to understand each other's underlying interests. | 8 |
| | 5. Work to establish a roughly equal balance of credits and debits in your collaborative accounts with your peers. | 8 |
| | 6. Build your influence through collaboration, not by accumulating or hoarding information or resources. | 9 |
| | 7. Recognize when you may have to sacrifice or contribute key resources for the good of the whole. | 9 |
| | 8. Focus on expanding the size of the pie and not just getting the biggest slice for yourself. | 9 |
| | 9. Keep your emotions in check by responding rather than reacting to input or actions you don't agree with. | 10 |
| | 10. Be willing to choose an effective outcome with your peers over the desire to demonstrate that you're right on a particular point. | 10 |

| Situation | Solution | Chapter |
|---|---|---|
| Getting a new boss | 1. Prepare yourself to share points of view that add quality to the executive conversation and decision-making process. | 2 |
| | 2. Trust your gut and speak up when you believe a poor decision is about to be made. | 2 |
| | 3. Establish a process of regular communication with your boss that enables easy and effective information exchange. | 4 |
| | 4. Create opportunities to speak for the good work of your team and position your boss to share that information with his or her peers and boss. | 4 |
| | 5. Share your results in a context that enables other executives to understand the progress made and the challenges overcome. | 4 |
| | 6. Do your homework before important presentations by learning what is most important to the audience and the methods of communication that work best for them. | 4 |
| | 7. Look to your boss for a clear definition of what to do, not an explanation of how to do it. | 8 |
| | 8. Keep your emotions in check by responding rather than reacting to input or actions you don't agree with. | 10 |
| | 9. Be a part of the group that works together to get things done when others are waiting for direction. | 10 |

# INDEX

Abbott, Cathy, 44–45, 50–51, 94,
    138–139, 144, 164–165, 167,
    170–171, 175–176
accountability: empowerment and,
    132–133; problem solving and, 128;
    responsibility vs., 8–9, 119–120
accountability model: description of,
    120; implications of, 125–129
achieving results, 22
affiliative leadership style, 67
Ailes, Roger, 184
Alziari, Lucien, 31–32, 89–90, 93,
    95–96, 100, 110, 116–117, 127–128,
    165
ambassador role, 177, 184
appearances, 186
arenas of life, 55–56
Aristotle, 21, 47

attire, 186–187
audiences: aligning of, with outcomes,
    62–64; preparing for, 77–78; types
    of, 63

Bailey, Joseph, 153
being comfortable, 24–26, 30
being right, 183–184
big footprint: description of, 10–11,
    165, 174; expectations associated
    with, 187–188; impact of, 176–177;
    minding your message and,
    184–187; positive uses of, 181
bigger thinking, 165–166
blaming, 127
body language, 82
boss: communication with, 68–72;
    new, 211; perspective of, 109;

boss, *cont'd*
relationship with, 68–69, 211;
updating of, 71–72; work results
conveyed to, 71–72
Boyatzis, Richard, 152–153
Bricklin, Dan, 53
broadening of vision, 164
business dress, 186–187

Carey, Drew, 62–63
Carlson, Richard, 153
Carter, Martin, 41–42, 64–68, 154
case study, 4–13
CEO disease, 153
Cerrone, Stephen, 80–81, 101
Cerveris, Michael, 175
change: dealing with, 191–192; distributive, 208–209
Christopher, Bill, 78, 166
Ciampa, Dan, 95
clear thought, 50
coaching, 148
collaboration with peers, 146–149, 162
communication: and affiliative style of
leadership, 67–68; audiences for, 63;
body language in, 82; with the boss,
68–72; connection building and,
67–68; crispness of, 74–75; custom-
fit, 11–12; 63; dialogue and, 65;
informality of, 66; intentional, 62;
with peers, 80–81; scheduling time
for, 81–82; with senior executives,
72–76; solution-based, 75; strategic
approach to, 62–63; with team,
81–82; trust building through,
143–144; with the whole organization, 64–68
communication culture, 66
communication framework, 69
competence, 3
conclusions, 197–198
confidence: building of, 7–8, 21, 192;
demonstrating of, 20–21; description of, 7; in doing things differently, 27–38; grounded, 20–21; in
learning stance, 27; peer relationships and, 30–33; speaking up and,

36; trusting your instincts and,
37–38
conflict resolution, 152, 210
connection building, 67–68, 163–164
conscious competence, 3
conscious incompetence, 3
consciousness, 193
constructive action, 28–29
control: approach to battle for,
182–183, levers of, 114–115
conversations: debating in, 179–180;
domination of, 179–180; "thinking
out loud," 178–179
core characteristics: identifying of, 47;
routines to reinforce, 49
credibility, 144–146, 150
Csikszentmihalyi, Mihaly, 43

debating, 179–180
dialogue, 65
distributive change, 208–209
domination of conversations, 179–180
dress, 186–187

Effron, Marc, 88–89, 163, 183
ego, 89–90
80/20 rule, 98–99
electronic devices, 187
elevator speech, 74
empathy, 109
empowerment, 132–133
energy renewal, 12–13, 41–42
engagement, 25–26
ESP. *See* Executive Success Plan
ethics, 123
execution, 110–111
executive: accountability by, 127;
attire worn by, 186–187; blaming by,
127; collaborative, 147; constructive
action by, 28–29; contributions by,
108–109; effectiveness vs. being
right, 183–184; engaging in new
activities, 25–26; expectations for,
173–174; feedback given to, 153;
first-time, 202; higher profile of.
*See* high profile; inside-out view by,
171; insight sharing by, 167; path

for, 182; persuasion by, 140–152; presence as leader, 82–83; problem solving by, 188; promotion of, 202; publicity associated with, 175–176; reframing your definition of work, 121–122; results achieved by, 126–127; self-sacrifice by, 163. *See also* senior executive(s)

executive level role: big-footprint view of. *See* big footprint; case study of, 4–13; changes associated with, 9; definition of, 2; expectations of, 161; focus in, 159–160; overview of, 1–2; requirements for, 2–3; transitioning to, 2–3

executive peers, 30–33. *See also* peers

executive presence, 15

Executive Success Plan (ESP): creation of, 195–199; description of, 13, 22

executive team, 9. *See also* team

exertion and recovery cycle, 42–43

expectations: big-footprint role and, 187–188; changing of, 173–174; at executive level, 161; setting of, 112–113

external networking, 171

feedback: analyzing of, 197; conclusions from, 197–198; description of, 101, 142; in Executive Success Plan, 195–199; inviting of, 180–181, 197; negative, 155; openness to, 153, 155, 180–181; soliciting of, 195–199

feedback team, 196, 198

first-time executive, 202

Flores, Fernando, 101

flow, 43

focus: broadening of, 166; at executive level, 159–160; on results, relationships affected by, 53–54; outcomes-related, 98, 120

Fuchs, Sid, 26, 92, 176

functional proficiency, 128

function-centric behaviors, 160–161

Gallwey, Tim, 33–34, 109–110

goal shaping, 100

Goleman, Daniel, 152–153

Good, Mary, 101, 107, 116, 138

grounded confidence: being comfortable and, 24–26; change and, 24–27; description of, 20–21; engagement and, 25–26; importance of, 32; operating at your best and, 23–24; relationship management and, 22–23

GRPI, 99–100

guideline setting, 114

Heifetz, Ron, 12, 44

high profile: ambassador role, 177, 184; domination of conversations, 179–180; examples of, 175–177; feedback, 180–181; living with, 175–181; others with, living with, 181–184; sense of humor, 177–178; "thinking out loud" conversations, 178–179

high-potential leaders, 116

hoarding of resources, 161–162

humor, 177–178

"I'm right" syndrome, 183–184

Immelt, Jeff, 169

incompetence, 3

information sharing, 168

inner critic: description of, 33; ego vs., 89

insecurity, 19–20

insight sharing, 167

instincts, trusting of, 37–38

interdependence, 140

interference, 33–35

interpersonal norms, 100

introverts, 36–37

Jeffay, Jason, 22–23, 80–81, 108, 115

Johnson, Bob, 24–25, 129–132, 177, 181

key issues, 74

King, Martin Luther, Jr., 80

Kotre, John, 53

Lanier, Mike, 29–30, 73, 77–78, 89, 111, 126, 189

leaders: development of, 115–116; giving up control by, 114–115; high-potential, 116; involvement of, 106–108; manager vs., 124; operating at their best, 23–24; people associated with, 92–93; presence as, 82–83, 101; value added by, 96
leadership: accountability by, 127–128; affiliative style of, 67–68; challenges of, 94; path of, 182
learning continuum, 2–3
Levy, David, 54, 149, 152
life course, 56–57
Life GPS: arenas of life, 55–56; benefits of, 46–47; core characteristics, 47; description of, 192; life course recalibrations using, 56–57; mental domain, 49–51; physical domain, 49, 52; relational domain, 49, 53–55; repeat behaviors to reinforce your best, 47–48; spiritual domain, 49, 52–53
Linehan, Steve, 31, 97–98, 112–113, 116
listening, 73
Loehr, Jim, 42
Lord, Al, 28
Lucas, Henry, 123–124

manager, 124
Marmer, Jay, 146–147, 149–150, 169
McCall, Morgan, 116
McDermott, Paul, 91, 188
McKee, Annie, 152–153
McKee, Robert, 80
"me mind-set": broadening of vision and, 164; connection building and, 163–164; description of, 160; hoarding of resources and, 161–162; overcoming of, 160–165; small-minded thinking and, 162–163
Mehrabian, Albert, 82
Meloy, Catherine, 188
mental domain, 49–51
message, 184–187
mind-set: "me." *See* "me mind-set"; "them," 168–171; "us," 165–168

Morea, Donna, 23–24, 64, 75, 100, 140–142

needs-based selling, 73
negative feedback, 155
negative self-talk, 35
network building, 154
networking, 171
Neustadt, Richard, 140–141
new company, 204–205

Okun, Arthur, 97
Olle, Laura, 161, 163, 176
open communication culture, 66
open-ended questions, 69, 73, 142, 167
organization: ambassador role in, 177, 184; executive's contribution to, 108–109; looking down into, 152–156; looking up in, 150–152; new, 204–205; outside-in perspective of, 168–169; representing of, 184–186
organizational presence: building of, 15, 196; field of vision and, 137–138
outcomes: audience aligned with, 62–64; clarity of, 63, 77; focus on, 98, 120; positive, 36; visualization of, 36–37
outside-in view, 10, 168–169
overwhelmed feeling, 206–207

peak performance: perspective and, 43–45; routines to enable, 45–46
peers: collaboration with, 146–149, 162; communicating with, 80–81; conflict with, 210; credibility with, 144–146, 150; equality with, 149–150; getting to know, 141–142; perceptions by, 189; relationships with, 30–33; trouble with, 210; trust building with, 143–144
performance: interference effects on, 33–35; potential and, 33
personal presence, 15, 196
perspective: expanding of, 166; keeping of, 57–58; of boss, 109; outside-in, 168; peak performance and,

43–44; renewal, 12–13; transposing, 109
perspective transference, 111–112, 167
persuading of others, 140–152
physical domain, 49, 52
Pittman, Bob, 104, 108
Plamondon, Bill, 108–109, 112, 130–131
political capital, 187, 189
positive impressions, 73–74
positive swing thought, 36
potential, 33
praise, 155
presence of leader, 82–83, 101
presentations to senior executives, 77–80
problem solving: accountability and, 128; executive's role in, 188; team-based, 100, 113
promotion, 203
publicity, 175–176

readiness assessments, 90–91
reciprocity, 149
Reich, Joni, 27–28, 155, 162
relational domain, 49, 53–55
relationships: with boss, 68–69; collaborative results and, 147; management of, 22
responsibility: accountability vs., 8–9, 119–120; ethics and, 123; monitoring of, 129; personal, 122–123
responsibility model: description of, 119–120; letting go of, 122–125
results: accountability for, 127; achieving of, 22; collaboration for building of, 146; 80/20 rule for, 98–99; by executive, 126–127; management of, 126; relationships affected by focus on, 53–54; short-term, 54; systems for monitoring of, 129–132
Rickover, Hyman, 106–107
Rippe, Steve, 105–106
routines: in mental domain, 49–51; peak performance, 45–46; in physical domain, 49, 52; reinforcing of, 49–55; in relational domain, 49,
53–55; setting up, 131; in spiritual domain, 49, 52–53; for thinking, 51
Russell, Bill, 57

Sannini, Ed, 35, 78–79, 94–97, 125–126
satisfice, 97
Schwartz, Tim, 42
self-awareness, 64
self-reliance, 87–88, 101, 103
self-sacrifice, 163
self-talk, 35
senior executive(s): communication with, 72–76; conflict resolution by, 152; positive impression on, 73–74; presentations to, 77–80; promotion to, 203; responsibilities of, 73; story-telling approach to, 79–80; work context explained to, 76. *See also* executive
sense of humor, 177–178
setting expectations, 112–113
setting guidelines, 114
sharing of information, 168
short-term results, 54
situation solutions guide, 201–211
small-minded thinking, 162–163
Smith, Steve, 125, 128, 141, 144–146, 160, 162, 164
solution-based communication, 75
solutions, 151–152
speaking up, 36
spiritual domain, 49, 52–53
Stavish, Mark, 27, 93, 100–101, 104, 147–148, 168, 170
Stephenson, Sue, 73, 168
Sterner, George, 106–107, 114–115, 122, 131–132, 154
strategic approach to communication, 62–63
strategic choice, 192
success: clarity of, 151; defining of, 109, 151; work results conveyed to boss, 71–72

team: asking people to leave, 95; broad-based, 189; communicating with, 81–82; competing with,

team, *cont'd*
91–101; different, 138–140; diversity of views in, 100–101; feedback about, 155; goal shaping by, 100; GRPI applied to, 99; "how" of task completion determined by, 106–108; members of, 92–93, 110; perspective transference to, 111–112, 167; praising of, 155; problem solving by, 100, 113; setting expectations with, 112–113; setting guidelines for, 114; staying grounded about, 155–156; value adding to, 96–99
team presence, 15, 196
team reliance: description of, 11, 87–89; right people in right roles for, 104–106, 110
"them" mind-set, 168–171
thinking: bigger, 165–166; routines for, 51; small-minded, 162–163
"thinking out loud" conversations, 178–179
transposing, 109

trust, 37–38, 101, 143–144
tunnel vision, 138

Ulrich, David, 69
unconscious competence, 3
unconscious incompetence, 3
"us mind-set," 165–168

value, 96–99
vertical tunnel vision, 138
vision: broadening of, 164, 166; expanding of, 166; organizational presence and, 137–138; vertical tunnel, 138
visualization, 36–37

Warren, Rick, 53
Watkins, Michael, 95
Welch, Jack, 169–170
work: context of, 76; facilitation of, 96; reframing your definition of, 121–122; results conveyed to boss, 71–72; value added to, 96–99

THE
EBLIN
GROUP

# NEXT LEVEL SERVICES FROM THE EBLIN GROUP

To support your organization's leaders in making a successful transition to the next level, The Eblin Group has developed the following services based on The Next Level model of executive presence:

### Keynote Presentations

Many organizations invite Scott Eblin to share his provocative point of view about what it takes to reach and succeed at the next level. Drawing on his "in the trenches" perspective as an executive, advisor to senior leaders, and author, Eblin provokes insight and action on what leaders need to pick up and let go of along the way.

### Executive Coaching and Advisory Services

The Eblin Group provides results-oriented coaching and advisory services to support executives in defining and acting on their most significant next level opportunities.

### Next Level Leadership™ Group Coaching

This program combines many of the benefits of individual coaching with the strength of a peer learning community to offer next level development to high-potential leaders. Offered at an economically efficient price point when compared to individual coaching, the program builds on the results of the Next Level Leadership Success Factor Survey™, an assessment deemed by 100 percent of past program participants to be either very applicable or highly applicable in helping them identify and act on their most important development opportunities.

### Life GPS® Coaching, Workshops, and Retreats

Building on the Life Goals Planning System (Life GPS®) outlined in Chapter 3 of this book, The Eblin Group offers Life GPS coaching, group workshops, and executive retreats to provide high-capacity leaders with a clear and succinct picture of how they are at their best, the routines that will help them reinforce peak performance, and the outcomes they can expect in the arenas of home, work, and community. The Life GPS provides leaders with unique and invaluable direction for living a next level life.

*For more information on The Eblin Group's next level services, call us at (888) 242-4680, e-mail us at info@eblingroup.com, or visit us at www.eblingroup.com.*